Of those to whom much is given, much will be required.

Jack remembered the words his mother had often repeated. Now he understood exactly what those words meant. A page had turned in Jack Kennedy's life. Gone were the days of carefree pranks, indifference toward studies, and reluctance to work hard. Jack was ready to meet all the demands that would come his way.

A Background Note about *John F. Kennedy*

After John F. Kennedy was shot and killed, his wife, Jackie, said, "Now he is a myth when he would rather have been a man." It has been nearly five decades since Kennedy was assassinated, yet he remains one of the most popular and fascinating Presidents in American history. Americans regularly vote Kennedy as one of the all-time best U.S. Presidents, along with such giants as George Washington and Abraham Lincoln.

Some may think of John F. Kennedy as a kind of storybook hero, like the king of Camelot, the mythical kingdom that Kennedy so loved reading about as a child. However, Kennedy was much more than the dashing young President with movie star looks and a beautiful wife who graced the covers of dozens of magazines. It's true that Kennedy enjoyed glamorous parties, sailboat racing, and fine cigars, but he was also a serious and thoughtful leader during a difficult time in United States history.

Although Kennedy was in office barely 1,000 days, he inspired a generation by creating the Peace Corps, pushing for a civil rights bill, and wisely choosing patience over anger when faced with the threat of nuclear war. Although Kennedy came from privilege and wealth, he was particularly concerned about helping poor people in the United States. In addition, Kennedy allowed himself to dream of the future, and he inspired the imaginations of millions when he began the work of putting a man on the moon.

An element of myth will always surround a man who made such a strong impression on so many and then died young. However, as you will discover in this book, John Fitzgerald Kennedy was a real man and, in many ways, an *ordinary* man who suffered, laughed, worked, and played like any of us. If he is remembered as something of a legend, it is, perhaps, due to the extraordinary heights to which he soared during his brief life.

JOHN F. KENNEDY

With
Chapters
on

BOBBY AND
TED KENNEDY

Tanya Savory

TP THE TOWNSEND LIBRARY

JOHN F. KENNEDY

TP **THE TOWNSEND LIBRARY**

For more titles in the Townsend Library,
visit our website: **www.townsendpress.com**

Illustrations © 2010 by Hal Taylor

All new material in this edition is
copyright © 2010 by Townsend Press.
Printed in the United States of America

0 9 8 7 6 5 4 3 2 1

Townsend Press, Inc.
439 Kelley Drive
West Berlin, NJ 08091
permissions@townsendpress.com

ISBN-13: 978-1-59194-217-7
ISBN-10: 1-59194-217-9

Library of Congress Control Number:
2009943314

TABLE OF CONTENTS

CHAPTER 1

In 1848, a farmer in Ireland named Patrick knelt on the ground and dug up a handful of potatoes that barely looked like potatoes. They were rotten—black and slimy—and they smelled terrible. A wave of fear shook the young man. A fungus had been spreading from farm to farm throughout Ireland for a few years, and now it had reached Patrick's land. Without his potato crop, he would die of starvation or sickness. Nearly one million Irish people had already died.

Knowing that staying in Ireland would be a dead end, Patrick decided to join the many thousands of people who were fleeing the country and boarding ships bound for the United States. Patrick had heard that America was a land of opportunity. Certainly, life would be better there than in Ireland. So Patrick spent his last bit of money to pursue this new dream.

However, the voyage to the United States was worse than Patrick's worst nightmare. The ships that carried the Irish emigrants were always terribly overcrowded, with hundreds of people crammed into the small, filthy, windowless areas beneath the deck. People who were already starving died quickly, as very little food was available for the passengers. Others died more slowly from disease during the month-long ocean journey. So many people passed away that the ships became known as "coffin ships"; it was said that sharks followed the coffin ships, waiting for the corpses that were tossed overboard daily.

Patrick made it to the harbor island near Boston, Massachusetts, alive. However, he didn't have even the two pennies needed to take the ferry to the city, so he remained on Noddle's Island (known today as East Boston) along with many of the other poor Irish emigrants. Home became one of the many dingy tenements that lined the muddy streets where garbage was piled high. Everywhere Patrick looked, Irish people suffered with sickness and poverty. This was not the dream Patrick had in mind when he had left his home far away across the Atlantic Ocean. Still, he moved forward, determined, against all odds, to one day become a successful man.

Finding even the lowest-paying work, however, was not easy. Although there were many jobs available in the shipyards, signs reading NO IRISH NEED APPLY were often posted right alongside the HELP WANTED signs. Patrick quickly found out that many Americans treated

Irish people unfairly, even cruelly, because of their religion. Most Irish were Roman Catholics, while most Americans were Protestants. Many Protestants did not agree with Catholicism and even believed that Catholics were evil and up to no good. Additionally, so many thousands of very poor, sick, and ragged Irish people had been pouring into Boston that some people unfairly stereotyped all Irish people as dirty and lazy.

In time, however, Patrick found a low-paying job making whiskey barrels on one of the docks. The job never paid enough for him to escape the slums of Noddle's Island, but he found happiness with a young woman named Bridget, who had also moved to the United States from Ireland. Patrick and Bridget married and had four children: three girls and then a boy. However, Patrick's happiness was short-lived. When the boy was ten months old, Patrick, barely 35, died of cholera. Patrick's young wife and their four children were left nearly penniless, and his dreams of success were left unfulfilled.

More than seventy years after Patrick had died in the slums of East Boston, a young boy listened to the story of Patrick and his difficult journey. The young boy also lived in Boston, but he was surrounded by wealth and opportunity. It was hard for him to imagine a grown man having to nail whiskey barrels together to make a living, and even harder to imagine not having even two pennies for a short boat ride. But perhaps most difficult of all for this boy to imagine was the fact that Patrick had been his great-grandfather.

Although Patrick Kennedy's dream had not come true, his widow, Bridget, had worked hard to keep that dream alive. To support herself and her four children, she had worked cleaning houses for some of Boston's wealthy families. Through that job, she glimpsed a better life—a life she wanted for her own family, especially for her only son. In time, Bridget began working in a shop that sold paper and sewing supplies. Amazingly, after a few years, she was able to buy that thriving business—and she began selling groceries in the store as well. All of the children helped out in the store, and Patrick Joseph, or "P.J.," as Bridget's son was called, worked other odd jobs, too.

Knowing that education would be necessary for P.J.'s success, Bridget managed to find the money to send him to a Catholic school. By the time he was 14, however, P.J. felt he had learned enough. He then quit school and took a job loading heavy cargo onto ships for up to eighteen hours a day. It was tough work for a fourteen-year-old, but, several years later, it paid off—literally.

P.J. invested his money in a rundown saloon by the docks. He fixed up the saloon, treated his customers with fairness and friendliness, and, in time, had enough money to open two more bars, one in the fanciest neighborhood in Boston. P.J. invested his money wisely and started more businesses. Before he was the age his father had been when he had died, P.J. was a rich and well-respected man. That respect then led P.J. to success in politics. He was elected to five one-year terms in the Massachusetts House of Representatives and then to three two-year terms in the Massachusetts Senate. In one generation, the Kennedy men had gone from making whiskey barrels to making laws.

P.J.'s only son, Joseph, was no less ambitious. Often fueling Joseph Kennedy's ambition was his anger at being treated rudely because of his Irish heritage. At Harvard University, he was not allowed to join certain clubs, and more than once he caught classmates talking behind his back about how he didn't belong at such a good school. He was told to his face by one particularly snobbish classmate that he'd never amount to much.

Joseph did his best to ignore the taunting. Instead of focusing on his anger, he focused on the future. He was determined to become a millionaire and prove everyone wrong—and he did just that. Only a year out of college, he became the youngest bank president in the United States. Like his father, he knew well how to both save and invest money, and his fortune grew quickly.

Soon after his appointment as a bank president, Joseph was ready to start a family. He married Rose Fitzgerald, a young woman he had known since childhood. Rose's family history was similar to Joseph's. Her great-grandparents had also migrated to the United States from Ireland during the potato famine, and her father, John, nicknamed "Honey Fitz" because of his sweet nature, had, like Joseph's father, worked his way into politics. Honey Fitz served as the mayor of Boston for several years and also served in the U.S. House of Representatives.

In time, Rose and Joseph had nine children, one of them being the young boy who now sat and listened with amazement to the story of his ancestors. Born in 1917, he was their second child, and he had inherited his Grandfather Fitzgerald's name: John Fitzgerald Kennedy. John, or "Jack," as he was always called, had been born into a life of luxury and riches. There were fun trips to the family vacation homes in Florida and on Cape Cod. There were servants and maids who brought Jack whatever he needed. There was the promise of a secure future, the best education, the best clothes—the best of everything.

"But remember," Rose concluded, looking at her young son's freckled face and bright eyes, "of those to whom much is given, much will be required."

Jack had heard his mother say that many times; it was from the Bible. And though he wasn't completely certain what the sentence meant, Jack knew that he was expected to appreciate what he had, and he was expected to be the best he could be.

Sometimes, however, Jack did not exactly feel like he was living up to expectations.

From a very young age, Jack Kennedy had been a sickly boy. Rose Kennedy kept a file of index cards on which she kept track of her children's illnesses. But Jack was sick so often that his card was nearly full even before he started school. While most children had a few typical childhood diseases, Jack had them all: whooping cough, measles, chicken pox, bronchitis, German measles, ear infections, and the most dreaded disease of all—scarlet fever.

Many people, particularly children, died of scarlet fever, and when Jack came down with it, his parents feared the worst. In addition, so many people were sick with scarlet fever that there was no room for Jack at any of the hospitals. However, Jack's father, an important and well-known man, was able to make a few promises and ask a few favors, and eventually get his son a room in a good Boston hospital. Joseph Kennedy promised to donate half of his money to charity if Jack survived the illness.

Jack's parents, along with a Catholic priest, gathered at Jack's bedside. The priest performed last rites, feeling that Jack was certainly close to death, but Jack struggled and fought against the illness. Joseph visited his young son in the hospital every day, praying and trying to keep Jack's spirits up. Against all odds, Jack recovered. And, keeping his promise, Joseph gave half his money to a charity that provided free dental care to children in Catholic schools.

In the years that followed, Jack would continue to be sick with all sorts of ailments. He was ill so often that his younger brother, Bobby, would joke that any mosquito that bit Jack was taking a big risk since Jack's body always seemed to have one sickness or another floating around in it. Jack often sat in his bed when he was ill, watching his brothers and sisters play games and race around the yard. It was difficult for a young boy to be cooped up inside so much of the time, but Jack soon discovered an excellent way to escape the boredom: reading.

In particular, Jack liked books about adventures in faraway and mythical places. *Treasure Island*, *Peter Pan*, *Kidnapped*, and *The Jungle Book* were among his favorites. But perhaps his favorite of all was King Arthur and His Knights of the Round Table. This was the tale of a brave and noble king who wanted more than anything else to establish a kingdom where peace reigned and where good deeds and creative thought were encouraged and rewarded. Surrounding King Arthur were his loyal knights, the beautiful Queen Guinevere, and even an old magician named Merlin. For a time, life was good in the kingdom known as Camelot. But then the queen and one of King Arthur's knights fell in love, and along with that came Camelot's downfall.

Jack was particularly intrigued by the story of King Arthur, because no one had ever been entirely certain whether King Arthur was a real man or a mythical character. That mystery provided hours of thoughtful entertainment for Jack, and even today, the question is left up to the reader to decide. More often than not, friends and family visiting Jack when he was sick found him propped up in bed covered in books, his brow wrinkled with concentration as he read. This love of reading stayed with Jack even when he was well, and on more than a few occasions, he hid in the big house so that he could finish a book instead of doing what he was supposed to be doing.

"I often had a feeling his mind was only half occupied with the subject at hand, such as doing his arithmetic homework or picking his clothes up off the floor, and the rest of his thoughts were far away weaving daydreams," Rose Kennedy recalled of her young son.

When Jack was 10, his family moved from Boston to Riverdale, New York, to be closer to their father's work in New York City. The family also needed a bigger house. There were now five children: Jack; his older brother, Joe Jr.; and three younger sisters, Rosemary, Kathleen, and Eunice.

Growing up a Kennedy may have been considered a life of luxury, but it was not necessarily a life of ease. Around the dinner table, there could be no small talk or idle chitchat. Politics and current events dominated typical dinnertime conversation, and when the children were old enough to read, they were instructed to read *The New York Times* every morning so that they could participate in these nightly conversations. Joseph Kennedy was a strict and demanding father who, as Rose Kennedy explained, "liked the boys to win at sports and everything they tried. . . . he did not have much patience with the loser."

However, in spite of all of these serious expectations, at a young age Jack developed a sense of humor and a streak of mischievousness. Along with his older brother, Jack made up ridiculous songs about bugs, and he bellowed them out to the neighborhood. The two boys changed signs on restaurant doors from NO DOGS ALLOWED to NO HOTDOGS ALLOWED, and they stole desserts from their siblings' plates when no one was watching. Once, when his father was scolding everyone at the dinner table for spending money irresponsibly, twelve-year-old Jack looked around the table and told everyone to cheer up. Then, with great authority, he explained, "The only solution is to have Dad work harder." Even Joseph Kennedy had to laugh at that.

Jack quickly learned that the ability to make people laugh could come in handy—particularly when his father was involved. When Jack decided that he needed a raise in his allowance, he presented "Chapter 1" of a book he had titled *A Plea for a Raise*. Although Jack had written only the first chapter (all 150 words of it), he had already honored his father by including "Dedicated to my [father,] Mr. J.P. Kennedy" at the beginning. Following a semi-serious description of why he needed a bigger allowance ("I put in my plea for a raise of thirty cents for me to buy scout things and pay my own way more around"), Jack signed his masterpiece, "John Fitzgerald Francis Kennedy." "Francis" was a comic flourish to make his name look more important—it wasn't really part of Jack's name. Joseph laughed out loud.

And Jack got his raise.

CHAPTER 2

"**If** you study too much," twelve-year-old Jack Kennedy explained seriously to his mother, "you're liable to go crazy."

Jack was home visiting midway through his eighth-grade year at Canterbury, an expensive and exclusive boarding school in Connecticut. His mother just looked at him and shook her head. It had been Rose Kennedy's decision to send Jack to a school other than the one his older brother, Joe Jr., was attending. Joe Jr. was at Choate, another boarding school in Connecticut. Jack's father had wanted both boys to attend the same school, but Rose thought Jack needed a break from his brother.

All through his childhood, Jack had been in Joe's shadow. Although the boys were very close, they competed viciously in nearly everything from completing puzzles to throwing footballs. In sports, the skinny, often sickly, Jack could rarely outperform his brother. Joe Jr. was a natural athlete. He was tall and strong with the typical Kennedy drive to win any game he played. Jack was no less driven, but no matter how hard he tried, he could not beat Joe Jr.

Once, Joe and Jack decided to race their bicycles around the block in opposite directions. Whoever returned to the starting point first would win the race. As the two boys approached each other, neither would move aside. Joe, assuming Jack would not be brave enough to crash right into him, sped up to reach the starting point first. Jack may not have been as strong as his big brother, but he was no less determined or brave. He lowered his head and smashed head-on into Joe Jr. The older brother merely stood back up and brushed off a little dust. Covered in blood, Jack was rushed to the hospital for twenty-eight stitches. Joe had won again.

Jack and Joe Jr. were, in many ways, best friends, but the rivalry between them kept Jack on edge. Some biographies suggest that Joe taunted and bullied his younger brother, sometimes making fun and taking advantage of Jack's frail health. Making matters worse was Joseph Kennedy's treatment of his oldest son.

"Joe was the architect of our lives," Rose Kennedy once said, meaning that because Joe Jr. was the oldest boy, he would continue to build the Kennedy name and legacy. A high level of honor, respect, and encouragement was given to Joe Jr., particularly by his father. Jack never received the same support.

Joseph wanted winners, and Joe Jr. was exactly that. All through grade school, teachers, classmates, and coaches loved Joe Jr. In addition, he was a good student and one of the best athletes anyone had ever seen. Jack was different. He was a bit shy, likely to daydream and neglect his homework, and too thin to play football as well as his brother. So, when Jack was ready for junior high, Rose put her foot down. She could see that the constant comparisons to Joe Jr. were bothering Jack, and she insisted that he go to a different school for at least two years.

However, Jack's time at Canterbury was short-lived. Sick once again, this time with appendicitis, Jack returned home before finishing the first year. In the fall of 1931, against Rose's wishes, Jack was enrolled at Choate, two years behind Joe Jr. Joe had already made his mark, and the headmaster of Choate never failed to mention to Jack how wonderful he thought his big brother was. Jack knew he should take this as a compliment, but it only irritated him.

Perhaps Jack's irritation led to his sometimes questionable behavior at Choate. After Jack had been at the school only a few months, the headmaster sent a note to Rose Kennedy in which he asked, "How could two brothers be so unalike?" Jack kept his dorm room in a state of chaos with clothes thrown everywhere, dirty dishes piled up, and homework lost in the mess. When Rose had sent her son a crate of oranges, Jack had used them for target practice, throwing handfuls at passersby below his dorm window. Jack walked around in wrinkled shirts, his wild hair sticking out in all directions.

Jack's attention span in his classes was hit or miss. Because he loved reading and learning about other people's lives and the world around him, Jack did very well in English and history. However, subjects that required what he called "routine work," like math or languages, bored Jack. More than once, he was caught snoozing in these classes or gazing out the window at clouds. At the end of his first year at Choate, Jack had failed Latin and French and had barely passed algebra. He returned for summer school to raise his grades.

"Let me thank you for your interest and patience with Jack," Rose Kennedy wrote back to the headmaster after Jack's first less-than-remarkable year. "He has a very attractive personality—we think—but he is quite different from Joe."

Jack's "attractive personality" was not lost on those at Choate. Though he was shy at times, his warm smile and quick humor won him many friends. He was so likable that in spite of his sometimes lazy study habits, teachers spent extra time trying to help and encourage him. The headmaster eventually warmed up to Jack and genuinely appreciated how different he was from Joe Jr. Even the cooks at the school, who shot worried glances at this very thin young man, pulled him aside and stuffed cookies into his pockets for him to take back to his room.

And Jack's classmates loved him. Jack had a fondness for practical jokes, and he wasn't particularly worried about getting caught. Once, he organized a group of students to gather hundreds of pillows from their dorms. With Jack leading the way, all the pillows were then crammed into a student's room, filling it from the floor to the ceiling. As Jack and several others stood casually in the hallway, chatting and watching from the corners of their eyes, the student got the surprise of his life when he opened his door to find a wall of pillows facing him.

Another time, Jack sneaked into the room of the student council president (someone Jack thought was an unbearable snob) late at night. He turned up the student's radio as loud as it would go and tiptoed back to his own room. Because radios in those days took a minute or two to warm up, Jack was in his bed pretending to be asleep when the radio startled the student council president out of his skin.

By the time Jack was a junior at Choate,

Joe Jr. had graduated and had left for a year of study at the London School of Economics before heading to Harvard. Perhaps this newfound freedom from his brother's shadow inspired Jack to new heights of mischief. Maybe his circle of equally mischievous friends encouraged him to push the limits. In any event, while most of Jack's jokes and pranks were harmless, he found himself in a pretty good bit of trouble midway through his junior year.

"Boys who do not uphold the ideals of this school do not belong here," the headmaster of Choate often repeated at student assemblies. "There is no place for 'muckers' at our school."

"Muckers" was a word the headmaster liked to use to refer to boys who broke rules and intentionally "mucked up" things around them. The headmaster had a good reason to be stern about this. Most of the boys at Choate came from very wealthy families, and some, as a result, were inclined to be lazy or to think that the world revolved around them. These boys thought they should be allowed to do whatever they wanted. But the headmaster knew that this kind of mindset would lead only to a difficult and unhappy future.

All Jack and his friends knew, however, was that "muckers" was a hilarious word and that the headmaster was far too serious about it. Inspired by the humor of it all, Jack and his three best friends decided to form a group called "the Muckers." The "club," which met every evening in Jack's room, quickly gained new members and had as its motto "bucking the system." Although the Muckers made big plans for getting into trouble, they rarely carried out their ideas.

"The worst things Jack and I ever did at Choate were to keep a messy room and be late for classes," Jack's closest friend, Lem Billings, explained years later.

However, news of the Muckers club somehow reached the headmaster. He was not amused. He was even less amused when he heard that the club was making plans to bring in a big pile of horse manure to the yearly Spring Festivities dance. Jack, in particular, thought it would be funny to pose for pictures next to such an unusual addition to the decorations. More than likely, the Muckers, as usual, would not have acted on their plans, but this didn't matter to the headmaster.

"Will you please make every effort to come to Choate on Saturday for a conference we think a necessity," he asked in a telegram to Joseph Kennedy.

At the conference, much to Jack's dismay and embarrassment, the headmaster called for him to be expelled. Joseph Kennedy was in complete agreement with the punishment, as he was furious with his son. Luckily for Jack, others at Choate felt that expulsion was too severe. Teachers liked

Jack in spite of his wild streak. The punishment was reduced to probation.

Jack would be back at Choate for his senior year.

"I didn't know what I wanted to do, and I didn't do much of anything," John F. Kennedy would later recall of his years at Choate. "Why? I don't know."

Illnesses (fatigue, ear infections, unexplained weight loss, stomach bugs, and back pain) had kept Jack out of class nearly a third of his junior year. Filling rooms with pillows and generally goofing around hadn't helped either. Even though Jack settled down in his senior year and began taking school more seriously, his overall grades were not very good. He graduated in the bottom half of his class with a grade average of 73 for all four years at Choate.

How could it be, then, that Jack Kennedy, leader of the Muckers and a true believer in the idea that too much studying could drive one crazy, was voted "Most Likely to Succeed" by the Choate class of 1935? Some believe that Jack, in one final prank to top all pranks, had rigged the election. However, others believe that both Jack's classmates and his teachers saw a spark in him, an unusual warmth and charisma that drew people to him. Even the headmaster, who had certainly had his ups and downs with Jack

Kennedy, wrote on Jack's final report: "Jack has it in him to be a great leader of men, and somehow I have a feeling that he is going to be just that."

During his last year at Choate, Jack had often visited his younger sister, Kathleen, at her boarding school nearby. Nicknamed "Kick" by the Kennedy family because she reminded everyone of a spirited pony, Kathleen was very close to Jack. They shared the same sense of humor, love of books, and curiosity about people and the world around them. Even Joe Jr., the star of the family and everyone's favorite, had to admit that he was, apparently, not Kick's favorite. In a letter to Jack, Joe Jr. wrote: "Kathleen has a love and devotion to you that you should be very proud to have deserved. . . . She thinks you are quite the grandest fellow that ever lived."

So it was with some excitement that Jack and Kick traveled together, accompanied by their parents, to Europe in the fall of 1935. Kick was headed to a school in France, and Jack, following in Joe Jr.'s footsteps, planned to spend a year at the London School of Economics before starting college. Since this was before air travel was common, the Kennedys boarded a huge and luxurious ship for the journey across the Atlantic—quite a change from the coffin ship accommodations of their ancestors not even one hundred years earlier. Jack and Kick raced around the deck, taking in the sights and chattering about the passengers. Jack was not exactly thrilled to be headed toward a year of economics study, but he couldn't wait to be in Europe. History and foreign lands had always intrigued Jack, even if foreign languages hadn't.

However, less than two weeks later, Jack would be headed back home due to illness. This time, doctors had a difficult time figuring out what was wrong. Finally, labeling the illness a "blood disease" or a "type of leukemia," doctors ordered Jack to take it easy and stay in bed for several weeks. Jack was tired of being sick and taking it easy. Instead, he headed off to Princeton University. He had already missed a few weeks of classes, but he thought he could catch up.

It was a Kennedy family tradition to go to Harvard, but all of Jack's friends were headed to Princeton, so Jack had convinced his father to let him go there instead. Plus, Joe Jr. was already a football star at Harvard; perhaps Jack didn't want to have to live up to Joe's reputation once again at a new school. It may be difficult to imagine how Jack, with his very average grades and his indifferent attitude toward school, could have ever gotten accepted at *either* Princeton or Harvard. But it should be remembered that Jack's father was a rich and powerful man—it was not the first time, nor would it be the last, that

Joseph Kennedy would pull some strings to help his son Jack.

However, no amount of money could buy good health.

Once Jack reached Princeton, his mysterious blood disease continued to get worse. Suddenly, he was losing weight at a frightening rate, and his skin began to turn yellow. Jack's parents and doctors ordered him to return home, where he was hospitalized for two months. Again, last rites were performed by a Catholic priest as Jack slipped in and out of consciousness. And again, Jack lived, but doctors hovered nearby, constantly taking blood tests and shaking their heads.

"Took a peek at my chart yesterday," Jack wrote to his best friend, Lem Billings, "and could see that they were mentally measuring me for a coffin. . . . tomorrow or next week we attend my funeral."

Jack, of course, was being mostly sarcastic with that prediction. With proper care and rest, he grew stronger and stronger. By the fall of 1936, Jack's health was actually better than it had been in a long time. Inspired by how strong he felt, Jack decided to transfer to Harvard and try out for the football team. He was still determined to prove that he could be as good as his brother in *something*. Maybe, with enough work, he, too, could be a big football star at Harvard.

"You don't weigh enough," Joe Jr. told his

younger brother. "You're going to get hurt." Joe, in his senior year at Harvard, was far more concerned with protecting his younger brother than competing with him. Joe Jr. had been scared when Jack had almost died—as much as Joe enjoyed one-upping Jack and teasing him, he couldn't imagine being without him.

Jack refused to back down. He put everything he had into the football practices, and, even though he weighed only 149 pounds at six feet tall, he made the team. What Jack lacked in size, he made up for with enthusiasm. However, the coach ignored him and never put him into any of the games. Finally, near the end of the season when Harvard had a huge lead in a game, Jack walked up to the coach in the fourth quarter.

"Come on, coach, let me play," Jack begged.

For a moment the coach stared at the wiry kid with the freckled face and pleading eyes. "Who the hell *are* you?" the coach asked in all seriousness. Then he turned back to the game.

Jack Kennedy walked back to the bench and hung his head in shame and anger.

To a nineteen-year-old who desperately wanted to step out of the shadow of his big brother and into his own light, Jack felt as if he would never win. In the long run, winning or losing at sports would make no difference at all, but Jack couldn't see that.

"Jack was more fun than anyone I've ever known," a friend from Harvard later recalled, "and I think most people who knew him felt the same way about him."

"Joe Jr. really had everything, but Jack was warmer, nicer, and so much less self-centered," another friend remembered.

These were the qualities that mattered, that would lead Jack to greatness one day. Others saw these qualities vividly, but on the sidelines of the Harvard football field in 1937, Jack Kennedy saw himself only as a loser.

CHAPTER 3

Joe Jr. had been right—Jack got hurt. After being humiliated by the coach, Jack became more determined than ever. He practiced late into the afternoons and even after dark, asking friend after friend to throw passes to him. One evening, Jack was particularly tired, but he continued practicing. Suddenly, he fell awkwardly, wrenching his back badly. It was an injury that would worsen and continue to bother him for the rest of his life.

Jack refused to give up his dream of matching Joe Jr. in sports, however. Once his back went from severe to only nagging, Jack turned to swimming instead of football. Again, he made the team, but just as he was gaining respect as a good swimmer, Jack came down with a viral infection that put him in the university hospital for a month. When he got out of the hospital, Jack was too weak and thin to try out for any other sport. In desperation, Jack ran for class president, thinking that perhaps he could make his mark in a different way. But he got barely any votes.

In college Jack had been focusing all his energy on everything but his studies, and his very average grades reflected that. However, during his sophomore year, something changed in Jack. Perhaps he decided that it might make more sense to try living up to his own potential rather than living up to his brother's reputation. Jack slowly began looking at the big world around him rather than focusing on his own little world. Jack had always been interested in world politics and history, and his professors at Harvard recognized an unusual thoughtfulness and intelligence in Jack Kennedy's writing about affairs of the world.

Joseph and Rose were relieved to see their son finally settling into his studies. Jack's parents encouraged his interest in world politics by sending him and his friend Lem Billings on an extended trip through Europe in the summer of 1937. It was an unusual opportunity at an unusual time. Many European countries were teetering on the brink of war.

At first, however, Jack's primary concern was finding European girls to date. Before the trip, he had bragged to Billings that he could "get girls whenever I want," and now he was out to prove that to his best friend. It didn't take long.

"He spent a lot of time thinking about girls," Billings later said of young Jack Kennedy, "and he was incredibly successful with them." Though Jack had failed French in high school, he somehow communicated well enough with French girls to get dates right away.

As the trip progressed, however, Jack found more important things to concentrate on. Everywhere he and Billings traveled, they heard murmurings of preparations for war. Germany, in particular, was ready to make its move. Many Germans were still angry over how they had been treated when Germany was forced to surrender at the end of World War I, and for some time they had wanted revenge. Now, they had a new, dynamic leader. He spoke with passion and fury about how Germany would take over other countries in order to get more "living space." And he was determined to keep the German race strong by keeping it "pure." He would do this, in large part, by killing millions of Jewish people and other people he felt were unfit for the German line. This leader's name was Adolph Hitler.

Jack and Billings enjoyed most of their European vacation. France and Italy were fascinating countries where the people (including girls) were friendly and eager to chat with these two young American men. But things were different in Germany.

"We just had an awful experience there," Billings would later write. Everywhere, German soldiers marched, and German people saluted one another with the shout "Heil Hitler!" Jack sensed a dark coldness from the Germans; something dangerous was indeed brewing. Jack and Billings had an opportunity to see Hitler speak while they were in Germany, but the atmosphere felt so eerie and unsafe that they hurried to get out of that country instead.

Jack returned to the United States with an increased awareness of the world around him, and a deeper interest in foreign affairs. As a result, he finally declared a major at Harvard: government. Jack had no plans to enter politics, since his father had made it quite clear that Joe Jr., as the oldest son, would be the politician of the family. More than a few times, Joseph Kennedy talked about Joe Jr. some day becoming President of the United States. Jack knew that this dream did not extend to him. He figured, however, that he could use his degree in government to become a journalist or an author.

In 1938, Joseph Kennedy was appointed ambassador to Great Britain, so the family temporarily moved to London. By then, the Kennedy clan included nine children: two more girls, Patricia and Jean, and two more boys, Robert ("Bobby") and Edward ("Ted"). Jack had to finish up his junior year at Harvard, so he was the last to travel to London. Because his grades had improved so much, he was allowed to leave school early, giving him several months in England.

As a result of his father's position, Jack worked as an unofficial researcher during his months in London. The position was "unofficial" because Jack wasn't actually employed; it was just Joseph Kennedy's way of giving his son another opportunity. And Jack did not waste the opportunity. Ambassador Kennedy asked Jack to visit various European countries and take notes on how the countries were preparing for war. From France, Jack wrote that the war plans under discussion were "so damned complicated" that he could barely understand what was going on. From Poland, he noted that "the Poles will fight," and as he drove through Germany, Nazis threw bricks at his car when they saw the English license plates. The Germans, he pointed out dryly, seemed fairly ready to fight, too.

The only country that seemed to be dragging its heels in preparing for war was, oddly enough, England. Rather than focusing on getting its armies ready to fight Germany, England's leaders seemed more interested in trying to come to some sort of peaceful agreement with Hitler. In talks with British leaders, Hitler agreed to stop invading other countries, and Britain's prime minister proudly announced that there would be "peace for our time." But the British leaders were wrong. Hitler had no problem with looking someone directly in the eye and lying. Less than a year later, Germany invaded Poland.

When Jack returned to Harvard for his senior year, he used all the information he had gathered in Europe to write his senior thesis. Mostly, he focused on why England was so unprepared for war. The 150-page paper was a tremendous amount of work, and Jack was proud of the end result.

Joe Jr., however, was not impressed. "It did not prove anything," he said, handing the paper back to his brother after reading it.

Both Jack's professors and Joseph Kennedy thought otherwise. Joseph thought his son's paper was good enough to be published as a book, so he got in touch with some of his publishing contacts in New York. And not long after Jack graduated from Harvard in 1940, his paper was released as a book titled *Why England Slept*. Some people, including reviewers, suggested that the book had been published only because of who Jack Kennedy's father was. Some even hinted that Jack hadn't actually written the book himself.

Regardless of the criticisms, *Why England Slept* became a bestseller and sold more than 40,000 copies in the United States and England. Jack, barely out of college, was suddenly an internationally famous author. Finally, Jack had accomplished something that his older brother never had. Even so, Jack was modest about his accomplishment, shrugging his shoulders and saying that "except for luck," the book would never have amounted to anything.

"The only luck involved," a family friend noted, "was the fact that Jack was the son of the American ambassador to Great Britain."

Of those to whom much is given, much will be required. Jack remembered the words his mother had often repeated. Now he understood exactly what those words meant. A page had turned in Jack Kennedy's life. Gone were the days of carefree pranks, indifference toward studies, and reluctance to work hard. Jack was ready to meet all the demands that would come his way.

In 1941, the first of many personal tragedies struck the Kennedy family. Of the nine Kennedy children, only one constantly did poorly in school and seemed to have real behavioral problems. Rosemary Kennedy was the oldest girl and the sibling closest in age to Jack. However, she and Jack were never close. None of the Kennedy children were very close to Rosemary; she was difficult to get to know. Perhaps Rosemary had learning disabilities or was mentally challenged. She was able to read and write, but she never progressed mentally much past the age of 10.

By the time Rosemary was in her late teens, she began having violent mood swings that resulted in tantrums and loud outbursts. These grew worse and worse, and, finally, when Rosemary was 23, Joseph Kennedy took her to a special type of surgeon. This surgeon performed lobotomies. A lobotomy is a procedure where part of the brain is cut so that wild behavior no longer takes place. The surgeon assured Joseph that nothing else about Rosemary would change—only her mood swings.

However, *everything* about Rosemary changed. The surgeon cut too deeply into Rosemary's brain, leaving her completely mentally disabled for the rest of her life. Although Rosemary would live to be eighty-six years old, she could only babble like a baby and stare into space. She had to be fed, and she had to wear diapers. Joseph Kennedy was horrified. Hiding the truth from his family, he had Rosemary sent to an institution far away in Wisconsin. He simply explained that it was time for Rosemary, with her problems, to go to a special school. Of course, in time, Rose and the children found out what had actually happened, and it created pain and anger that were rare in the Kennedy household.

"I will never forgive Joe for that awful operation he had performed on Rosemary," Rose Kennedy said of her husband many years later. "It is the only thing I have ever felt bitter towards him about."

But as the Kennedys would have to do more than a few times, they moved forward from personal tragedy and tried to focus on the future. World War II was beginning to threaten, and though the United States had not yet entered the war, all of the armed forces were gearing up. Still, President Roosevelt was reluctant to declare war.

"To you mothers and fathers, I give you one more assurance," President Roosevelt had said earlier in the year. "Your boys are not going to be sent into any foreign wars!"

Joseph and Rose Kennedy hoped against hope that this would be true, but young men everywhere were already enlisting—and among them were Joe Jr. and Jack. For Joe Jr., being accepted into the military was no problem; he could enter whichever branch of service he preferred. Hoping to fly exciting missions, Joe chose the Navy's Aviation Cadet Program. He would certainly get his chance for excitement. This program was considered one of the most dangerous in the armed forces.

On the other hand, Jack's experience in the military was not, at first, very exciting at all. Because of his bad back from his football injury, and because he was so skinny from so many illnesses, Jack could not pass the physical exam. None of the branches of the military would accept him. Joe Jr. had won again! Jack spent the entire summer lifting weights to strengthen his back and eating many milkshakes in an attempt to gain weight. Meanwhile, Jack's father quietly pulled a few strings to help get his younger son enlisted. As much as Joseph Kennedy feared his sons fighting in a war, he knew that serving in the military was important to Jack.

Finally, Jack was accepted into the Navy and appointed to the Office of Naval Intelligence. Jack was instantly bored with his assignment. There was nothing very thrilling or dangerous about writing reports and being chained to a desk job. In an attempt to counteract the boredom, Jack began dating a woman that many friends and coworkers warned him not to date. Inga Arvad was from Denmark, but her connections to Germany, and even to Hitler himself, worried authorities in the United States. The FBI had been keeping an eye on this young woman, concerned that she might be a spy for the Nazis.

When the FBI discovered that Jack was dating Inga, he was threatened with a dishonorable discharge unless he stopped seeing her. Jack was in love, however, and he refused. Joseph Kennedy was furious with his son—a dishonorable discharge from the United States Navy would be a terrible disgrace to the Kennedy name! Again, Joseph pulled a few strings and had Jack transferred to Charleston, South Carolina, to put an end to the relationship with Inga. Jack was not happy with this arrangement, but it certainly ended the affair quickly.

"As you probably haven't heard," Jack wrote with some bitterness to Lem Billings not long after being sent to Charleston, "Inga got married—and not to me."

In the midst of all of Jack's romantic woes, Pearl Harbor was attacked by Japan, an ally of Germany. The attack caused the United States to officially enter the war, and Jack was given the opportunity to train to be a captain of a patrol torpedo boat. Captaining a patrol torpedo boat (commonly called a "PT boat") would not be quite as glamorous as what Joe Jr. was preparing to do, but at least Jack would see some military action. He jumped at the opportunity.

By April 1943, Jack had become a lieutenant and was in charge of his own boat: *PT-109*. He and his crew were based in the South Pacific near the Solomon Islands. His squadron's orders were to patrol at night and search for Japanese ships carrying military supplies. If Japanese ships were spotted, the PT boats would attack them and then speed away out of danger. PT boats were very fast because they were so light, but the lightness came with a significant drawback: PT boats were constructed of plywood. It took very little to sink one, and because the boats were packed with torpedoes and other explosives, they were like flimsy floating bombs.

Jack didn't worry too much about the danger. He was proud to be in charge of a boat, and he liked his crew. More often than not, the long nights of patrolling the channels between the islands were uneventful, but occasionally a Japanese ship would be spotted, and then Jack and his crew would attack the ship with torpedoes and strafe it with machine gun fire.

Then came the early-morning hours of August 2, 1943.

Unseen by Jack and his crew was an entire fleet of Japanese destroyers. Around 3:00 a.m., *PT-109*'s lookout saw what he thought was another PT boat approaching. It was a very dark, moonless night, so the lookout didn't realize that what he was seeing was only a small part of a huge destroyer. By the time he realized his mistake, it was too late.

"Ship at two o'clock!" came the frenzied shout of the lookout, who was indicating the other ship's position. Jack pushed his boat to full throttle and tried to steer away, but it was no use. The destroyer was practically on top of *PT-109*, and the Japanese ship plowed right on through the small plywood boat, cutting it completely in half. The lookout and another crew member were killed instantly. Jack was slammed against a wall, reinjuring his frail back, and was then thrown out of the boat into the dark ocean. As gasoline began burning on the water, Jack could hear the screams of other crew members.

"So," Jack thought, "this is how it feels to be killed."

CHAPTER 4

"Swim away from the boat! Swim away!"

Jack realized that he wasn't wounded badly, and as his vision cleared, he could make out several crew members treading water near the sinking wreckage. Jack thought it would be only minutes until *PT-109* blew up. Fiery water crept closer to the broken boat.

"Grab onto debris and swim out!"

For the rest of that night and into the next day, the eleven survivors held onto parts of the boat and waited for another U.S. Navy ship to come and rescue them. Hours passed, but no other friendly boats came through. Worried that the plywood debris would begin sinking, Jack told his crew that they would have to swim to the closest island, about four miles away.

"I can't," came the agonized voice of one of the men, Patrick McMahon. "I can't move at all."

Jack swam over to McMahon and realized that he was too badly burned to swim. Jack refused to leave any of his men behind. Although his back was in pain, Jack clenched the belt from McMahon's life jacket between his teeth, and swam for four hours, towing the injured man. Perhaps Jack Kennedy had never been a star athlete at Harvard, but all his determined hours on the football field and in the pool were now paying off.

When Jack and the crew reached the tiny island, they collapsed, exhausted. But Jack knew their only hope was to flag down a passing PT boat, so as soon as it got dark, Jack swam back out into the passage. He tied a revolver around his neck so that he could fire shots to get the attention of the passing boats. Jack waited for hours without seeing another boat, however. "Where is everyone?" Jack thought worriedly. PT boats were supposed to patrol the passage regularly. Finally, in disgust and some anger, Jack gave up. He returned to the island later that night to find many of the crew members in a sorry state—desperate for water, they had cracked open coconuts for milk, but the still-green coconuts had made them sick. The men had gone without water for more than eighteen hours.

In the morning, Jack made the difficult decision to swim to yet another island. Often, supplies were left on the islands for stranded boat crews, and Jack and the other men were in critical need of both food and water. Jack chose one of the strongest swimmers to go with him, and hours later the two men crawled onto the shore. To their great relief, there was a small chest filled with food, a container of fresh water, and a canoe to carry it all back to the other island.

As Jack and the other man paddled nearer to the island where they had left the rest of their crew, they saw a surprising sight: Several natives stood with the men, motioning with their hands in an attempt to communicate. The crew members had been unwilling to explore the island for fear of running into Japanese soldiers, but the friendly natives had discovered the desperate crew and were trying to help them. Once on shore, Jack came up with a plan for being rescued. Picking up a coconut and pulling out his pocketknife, Jack carved this message on the shell:

NATIVE KNOWS POSIT [position]
HE CAN PILOT BOAT
11 ALIVE
NEED SMALL BOAT
KENNEDY

He handed the coconut to the natives and communicated that he needed them to take it to nearby Rendova Island, where Allied troops were stationed. The natives left quickly in their canoes, and the next evening, a PT boat finally picked up Kennedy and his stranded crew.

"Where *were* you guys?" Jack asked angrily, explaining that he had waited for hours in the channel and had never seen one boat. The other captain shrugged. It was possible, after all, to have missed one another in the wide channels. As an apology, the captain offered Jack food, but, still a little irritated, Jack waved off the food at first and said sarcastically, "No thanks. I've just had a coconut."

Within days, Jack Kennedy was a national hero who would be awarded both the Purple Heart Medal and the Navy and Marine Corps Medal. News of his bravery and quick thinking spread from coast to coast, and stories appeared on the front pages of *The New York Times* and all the Boston papers.

To Jack's way of thinking, he had only been doing his job. He felt a bit embarrassed by all the attention, and was determined to remain unchanged by fame. Apparently, he was successful. "He still is late at meals—he still is vague on his plans—he still overflows his bathtub and ruins my bedroom rug," Rose Kennedy reported about her entirely unchanged son.

And years later when a young boy asked Jack how he had become a war hero, Jack just smiled and said, "It was easy. They cut my boat in half."

Even Joe Jr. had to admit that he was truly impressed by his brother's courage and sent Jack a letter both congratulating him and, competitive to the end, announcing, "I shall return home with the European Campaign Medal if I'm lucky."

Joe Kennedy, Jr. would not be lucky.

In August 1944, Joe Jr. was scheduled to return home from the war in Europe. By then a pilot in the Army Air Force, Joe had already flown some fairly risky missions, and the Air Force decided it was time to give the young pilot a much-needed break. But Joe said no. There was an extremely dangerous mission that needed volunteers, and Joe was the first in line to sign up. Perhaps he wanted to even the "hero" score with his brother. Perhaps he simply wanted to serve his country in the bravest way he could.

In any event, instead of returning home, Joe was strapped into a plane that was carrying more than 20,000 pounds of explosives. The plan was to pilot the plane to the English Channel and then set it on autopilot to continue on to Normandy, France, where the bombs would be dropped on German troops. Joe Jr. was to bail out over the channel, parachuting to the water below, where he would be picked up. When a friend jokingly asked Joe, right before he took off, whether he had insurance, Joe just grinned and said, "Nobody in my family needs insurance."

It was a plan that had worked before, but this time something went terribly wrong. Joe's plane suddenly exploded in midair, killing him instantly.

The flash from the explosion was so bright that it momentarily blinded pilots flying half a mile away. Joe Kennedy, Jr., would indeed be a war hero, but at the greatest cost imaginable.

The Kennedys were devastated. And while Jack had had his disagreements with his older brother, there was, perhaps, no one that he had admired more. Jack received the news while he was in the hospital recuperating from an operation on his ever-ailing back.

"I don't know anyone with whom I would rather have spent an evening or played golf or, in fact, done anything," the grieving Jack wrote from his hospital bed to a friend. "Joe was the star of our family. He did everything better than the rest of us."

Upon entering the Air Force, Joe Jr. had written something about his younger brother, too. "As far as the family is concerned," he had written to his father, "it seems that Jack is perfectly capable to do everything, if by any chance anything happened to me."

Jack was well aware of what his brother had meant by "everything." All of their parents' hopes and dreams had been pinned on Joe Jr. Joe was destined to go into politics as both his grandfathers had done. He was to achieve greatness—there was even talk of him being President some day. With Joe Jr. gone, all the family dreams fell to

Jack. At first, Jack was reluctant to enter politics. He was still rather shy, and he had no desire to stand up in front of crowds and talk about himself in order to get votes.

"I was always interested in writing," Jack would later explain. "I wanted to teach for a while. . . . The war really changed my life, and I suppose if it hadn't been for that and what happened then, I would have gone on with my original plan."

At first, Joseph Kennedy did not force Jack to enter politics, but he hinted at it quite frequently. As a result, Jack struggled to decide what he should do with his future. After completing his commitment to the Navy, he briefly attended graduate school at Stanford University in California, studying economics with the idea of going into business. This lasted less than a year, however, when Jack found himself hospitalized yet again with back problems. Next, Jack worked as a writer, covering the first meetings of the United Nations in San Francisco.

However, his father's pressure to enter politics progressed from hints to clearly voiced expectations.

"It was like being drafted," Jack later explained. "My father wanted his eldest son in politics. 'Wanted' isn't the right word. He *demanded* it."

As Jack began adjusting to the idea of being

a politician, World War II finally came to an end. The war in Europe pretty much ended by the spring of 1945. Seeing that he would not win, Hitler committed suicide in April, and then Germany surrendered a week later.

However, Japan refused to surrender. President Truman, who had become President after Franklin Roosevelt had died suddenly, set forth demands for surrender, but they were ignored by Japan. Finally, under a lot of pressure from the secretary of defense, Truman made a dark and difficult decision.

On August 6 and August 9 of 1945, atomic bombs were dropped, first on the Japanese city of Hiroshima and then on the port city of Nagasaki. The residents of the cities had received no warning of the attack. As the Japanese civilians went about their regular morning activities, an explosion unlike any explosion ever witnessed on the face of the earth reduced two bustling cities to barren wastelands.

The mushroom cloud from each bomb rose eleven miles into the sky. It was estimated that more than 120,000 people were killed instantly, many of them leaving nothing more than a shadow of dust, the outlines of their bodies, on the ground. Many thousands more died later from injuries and diseases resulting from radiation. One reporter walking around Hiroshima the day after the blast described the city by saying, "Everything that burns was burned. . . . The whole city became extinct."

It was the first and, hopefully, the last use of nuclear warfare. Japan surrendered, and those who supported the use of the atomic bombs argued that if the war had dragged on and the Allies had had to invade Japan, even *more* people—several million, in fact—would have died. Use of the bombs was, they claimed, a necessary evil. Still, many people felt the bombs were an *un*necessary evil. One of them was Dwight Eisenhower, who had served as Supreme Commander of the Allied forces in Europe during World War II. Nearly twenty years after the war, and after Eisenhower had served two terms as President of the United States, he told *Newsweek* magazine, "The Japanese were ready to surrender, and it wasn't necessary to hit them with that awful thing."

Still, days after the bombs were dropped, World War II ended, and Americans celebrated a victory.

In Boston, Jack Kennedy began working toward a victory of his own. He had finally sat down with his father and discussed running for office, and father and son had agreed that running for the House of Representatives would be Jack's best bet. Furthermore, a seat in the Eleventh Congressional District of Massachusetts had just opened up.

The Kennedy name was certainly known in the Eleventh District, but in many ways, it was an odd congressional seat for Jack to pursue. That section of Boston contained factories and slums, and was home to blue-collar workers. The bars and streets were full of what Joseph Kennedy described as "hard-boiled guys" who would have nothing in common with a rich, Harvard-educated kid like Jack Kennedy. In fact, it seemed that Jack's wealth and privilege would be a serious strike against him. Making matters worse, Jack really *did* still look like a kid. At 29, he had the skinny, freckled, tousled-hair appearance of a teenager. The tough guys in this district would eat him alive.

Joseph Kennedy considered all this and shook his head. He would not have worried about Joe Jr., but Jack was quiet and uncomfortable in front of a crowd. He was uneasy with the backslapping, handshaking, and forced laughter required of every politician. How on earth would Jack win the support of the rough, working-class crowd of the Eleventh District?

"My name is Jack Kennedy; I am a candidate for Congress. Will you help me?"

Maybe more than a thousand times, Jack walked up to total strangers in the Eleventh District and introduced himself that way. In the tenements, on the street corners, in the rowdy bars, and out along the docks with the burly longshoremen—Jack Kennedy was seen everywhere. What he might have lacked in powerful speechmaking (his speeches at that time were described as "wooden" and "lifeless"), he more than made up for with his genuine interest in people. Jack was not just trying to get votes; he was really trying to get to know the people he hoped to represent. It was not unusual for Jack to sit down and chat with people for an hour or more.

Worried about his son's campaigning skills, Joseph Kennedy once secretly followed Jack down to the docks. A group of tough dockworkers turned to stare coldly at Jack as he approached. Jack walked right up to them and introduced himself, asking for their votes. Joseph watched, with amazement, as Jack continued to talk and all of the men began to smile. Within minutes, the dockworkers were laughing and, whether Jack liked it or not, slapping him on the back.

"I never thought Jack had it in him," Joseph Kennedy would later admit. "But I didn't worry about him after that."

Joseph Kennedy may not have worried about Jack after that, but he was always involved during the campaign. Not only did he make certain that everything was very well funded, he also made his opinions and wishes very well known. At times, Jack found his father to be overbearing and even embarrassing. However, it is probably true that Jack would not have stood much of a chance in the campaign without the generous financial support from his father. Joseph Kennedy liked to repeat a motto he had learned from an old politician friend: "It takes three things to win. The first is money and the second is money and the third is money."

However, it wasn't just the power of money that helped Jack gain popularity in the Eleventh District. The power of the Kennedy family all working together to get Jack elected both amused and charmed many voters. The devotion of Jack's younger brothers and sisters to their oldest sibling's success was moving. Twenty-year-old Bobby kept the campaign headquarters in order and shook hundreds of hands as he said, "I'm Robert Kennedy, and I sure hope you'll support my brother John." Fourteen-year-old Ted ran errands, handed out leaflets, and even played softball with the kids in the Eleventh District.

Jack's sisters, along with their mother, hosted what would become famously known as the "Kennedy teas." To these tea parties, the Kennedy women invited many of the important, well-known, and highly respected women of the community. Rose Kennedy, then, would tell funny stories about Jack. She'd pull out the old index card with all his ailments and read the long list. She'd pass around childhood pictures of him with his ears sticking out and his hair a mess. Rose knew that if these women could see Jack as a real person and not just a politician, they would be more likely to vote for him.

Although Jack was new to campaigning and was often uncomfortable with it, he had a great gift of connecting honestly with people. His sense of humor, particularly his ability to poke fun at himself, won over many of the voters who had assumed that, because of his wealth, Jack would be a self-centered snob. Jack was sincere and looked people in the eye when he talked to them. Instead of bombarding voters with information about himself, he would often simply ask, "Do you have any suggestions?"

Joseph often grew frustrated with his son's reluctance to brag about being a war hero. To Joseph Kennedy, this seemed to be the most important piece of information his son could use to sway voters. But Jack didn't see it that way at all. To Jack, there were many young men who had been much more heroic than he had been—the ones who had given their lives were the ultimate heroes. Joseph then encouraged Jack to talk about how he had lost a brother in the war, but Jack said no. Using his brother's death to gather votes seemed even worse.

Near the end of his campaign, Jack made a special effort to speak to a group of a few hundred Gold Star Mothers. Gold Star Mothers were women who had lost a son in the war, and there were many of them in the Eleventh District. Perhaps these women assumed that Jack Kennedy would talk about his own experiences in the war, but he didn't. Shyly and somewhat awkwardly, Jack looked around the room.

"I think I know how you feel," the young candidate said quietly, "because my mother is a Gold Star Mother, too."

Afterward, the women gathered around Jack with tears in their eyes, hugging him.

"He reminds me of my own son," one of the mothers said to another.

In November 1946, John F. Kennedy was elected to Congress, representing Massachusetts's Eleventh District.

CHAPTER 5

"Son, could you run and get us a few of today's newspapers?" an older congressmen asked Jack on one of his first mornings in Congress. Jack looked confused for a moment, and then he grinned with slight embarrassment.

"I'm not a page," Jack explained. "I'm a congressman from Massachusetts."

It would not be the only time that Jack Kennedy would be mistaken for a congressional page or an elevator operator because of his youthful appearance. It wasn't just Jack's young face. More often than not, he showed up in a wrinkled shirt and mismatched socks, and with wild hair. Occasionally, if he had run out of clean suits, he'd wear a tux jacket with khaki pants. Although Jack had been raised in a wealthy atmosphere, neither fashion nor neat appearance was a particularly big concern of his.

However, Jack *was* concerned when other congressmen refused to take him seriously. Sometimes when he tried to argue his opinion, he was interrupted. Other times, he was simply ignored. In addition to thinking that Jack was too young, some of the other congressmen thought that Jack was only supporting his father's views. And while it was true that Jack didn't always know a lot about some of the issues, he was certainly not just a puppet for his father's political ambitions. In fact, Jack often argued with Joseph Kennedy about votes in Congress that had to do with foreign policy. Once, at a garden party in Washington, D.C., a reporter was thrilled to witness Jack stand up to his father and sternly say, "Now, look here, Dad, you have your political views and I have mine. I'm going to vote exactly the way I feel I must on this."

Now living in Washington, D.C., Jack spent a lot of time learning the ropes of being a politician and learning about life in Washington. He rented a small house in the Georgetown area of the city and did his best to socialize with all the important people. However, scoring popularity points with other politicians was not Jack's favorite social pastime. Making good impressions on single women—lots of single women—was considerably more appealing to the young congressman. Women continued to find Jack irresistible, but Jack wasn't looking for anything long-term.

"I was more interested in more serious relationships," said one woman he dated during that time. "But he was flirtatious, and he liked flirtations."

Of course, as a member of the House, Jack Kennedy had a lot of things to do other than find dates. During his three two-year terms, Jack was particularly interested in social issues, such as affordable housing for war veterans. He also pushed for fair wages, more jobs, and increased Social Security for senior citizens. However, as a junior representative in a legislative body that had over 400 members (nearly all of them older and with more seniority), Jack didn't have much pull. And as had sometimes happened years ago at Choate, Jack found the repetitive and routine work of a congressman boring. Worst of all, he often felt that congressmen were not very important and that they never made much of a difference.

"We're just worms," Jack once said of the House of Representatives. "Nobody pays much attention to us nationally."

After six years in the House, he was ready for something different.

Before leaving the House, two events took place in Jack Kennedy's life—neither of them happy. In 1948, upon returning home after a dinner party, Jack received some terrible news about his favorite sister and close friend, Kathleen "Kick" Kennedy. Four years earlier, Kick had married a British army officer, a man she had fallen in love with while working for the Red Cross during the war. However, only four months after being married and less than a month after Joe Jr.'s plane had exploded, Kick's new husband was killed by a sniper during military action in Belgium.

And now another tragedy: Kick had died in a plane crash in France. This string of deaths, closely preceded by the disastrous lobotomy operation on Rosemary Kennedy, started what has come to be known as the "Kennedy Curse." In the years to come, an unusual number of other Kennedys and close Kennedy relations would die young from unnatural causes. Some people began to think that some kind of curse or hex had been placed on the Kennedy family. Of course, the idea of something mysterious preying on the Kennedys is based on imagination, and there is no way to prove it. Still, the idea has fascinated the American public for decades and has been the subject of numerous articles, books, and even television programs.

Next, while still reeling from the news about his sister, Jack became ill again. He was barely able to eat anything without it upsetting his stomach. Jack had always been thin, but now he was becoming dangerously gaunt. His skin tone again turned yellowish, and he finally reached a point where he could not get out of bed without collapsing from fatigue. One doctor who examined him said, "He hasn't got a year to live."

Just in the nick of time, Jack was diagnosed with Addison's disease, a hormone illness that, luckily, could be treated with drugs. Still, doctors were not at all sure that Jack would survive. The disease had taken its toll. "Jack was sick or in pain," brother Bobby would later recall, "at least one half of the days he spent on this earth." However, Jack seemed to respond well to the medications. During Jack's hospitalization, Joseph Kennedy went to great lengths to hide from the public just how sick his son was—he knew that an image of illness would not be good for his son's political career.

And Jack's career was about ready to take off in a big way.

"It was those damn tea parties that beat me!"

Senator Henry Cabot Lodge, Jr., smiled and shook his head. It was November 1952, and he had just lost the Senate race in Massachusetts to John F. Kennedy. Again, Jack's campaigning had been a family affair. Rose and her daughters had hosted no fewer than thirty-three teas, with Rose learning a bit of French and Italian to charm voters in certain ethnic neighborhoods.

Rose also took it upon herself to watch Jack more closely during this race and give him advice. "Take your hands out of your pockets when you're speaking," Rose once instructed, claiming that it made Jack look unsure of himself. She also suggested that he wear only black shoes ("they make you look more grown up") and maybe a striped tie now and then, since Lodge wore striped ties.

No one had thought that Kennedy could beat Senator Lodge. In the entire history of Senate races in Massachusetts, Democrats had won only twice. In addition, Lodge was fifteen years older than Kennedy and a seasoned two-term senator. Even more important, Lodge was a Republican who had close ties to Dwight Eisenhower, the popular Republican candidate for President. Everyone assumed that Lodge would triumph easily.

However, Jack Kennedy had a strong desire to win. Six years earlier, as he had entered the campaign for Congress, he wasn't entirely certain he even wanted to be in politics. After Joe Jr. had died, Jack had felt obligated to fulfill his father's dream for the oldest son. Gradually, however, succeeding in politics was becoming Jack's goal, too. The House of Representatives had not given Jack many opportunities to make changes or voice his opinions, and he wanted to become a senator specifically so that he could have those opportunities.

One issue that particularly interested Kennedy was the growing threat of Communism throughout the world. In Communist countries, free enterprise and private ownership do not exist. Everyone, in theory, does the same amount of work for the same amount of pay and goods. In some ways, this may not sound like such a bad idea. However, the government in Communist countries has both ownership and control of nearly everything, so individuals cannot own a home or a business. Many people worry that when a government controls everything and makes everyone's lives essentially the same, individual excellence disappears. In other words, without competition—and without the rewards for being better than someone else at something—everyone becomes merely average. In the 1950s, Americans were very concerned about Communism, perhaps more than about any other international issue.

To become more familiar with the threat of Communism, Kennedy traveled to both European and Far Eastern countries in the two years leading up to his senatorial race. Many Americans had vague ideas about what was happening in other parts of the world, but Kennedy wanted to see things firsthand. Voters, both Democrat and Republican, admired the young candidate's commitment to learning the truth. Slowly, he began to win voters away from Lodge.

As always, Joseph Kennedy's seemingly endless financial support didn't hurt Jack's campaign either. However, in this campaign, Jack was firm about asking his father to remain behind the scenes. He wanted voters to see him as a strong, real politician, and not just the son of the rich and powerful Joseph Kennedy. Some reporters still tried to present Kennedy as a spoiled kid whose daddy bought him anything he wanted—even political offices. Kennedy was determined to erase this image.

On the other hand, Jack brought his brother Bobby out from behind the scenes and made him his campaign manager. This proved to be a wise move. Bobby was fiercely dedicated to Jack and was willing to do anything necessary to help Jack succeed. Sometimes described as ruthless, Bobby did and said whatever he needed to do or say to get the job got done.

"If you're not going to work," he often barked at lounging campaign workers, "don't hang around here."

Reporters rushed to get pictures and interviews with this fiery twenty-seven-year-old Kennedy. Although Bobby was often shy and nervous when forced to give a speech, he was quick to speak his mind in informal settings. When he was asked about his short temper, Bobby waved the question away and explained, "I don't care if anybody around here likes me, as long as they like Jack."

Due to their eight-year age difference, Jack and Bobby had never been close growing up. However, they formed a very strong bond during the race for the Senate. It was a bond that would last the rest of Jack's life.

For nearly three years, Jack Kennedy campaigned. Often he was in tremendous pain. After the football injury and the war injury, Kennedy's back had gotten so bad that he was forced to use crutches much of the time. He seldom used the crutches when he was campaigning, however, wanting voters to have the image of him as a strong man. Kennedy simply endured the pain as he attended events and gave speeches. He was well aware of how his handsome and youthful image attracted voters—particularly female voters.

"What *is* there about Jack Kennedy that makes every Catholic girl in Boston between 18 and 28 think it's a holy crusade to get him elected?" Lodge's frustrated campaign manager once asked.

Of course, it wasn't just "Catholic girls in Boston" that rallied for Kennedy. Statewide, Kennedy had shaken hands with more than 100,000 people. The evening before the election, as Bobby drove himself and Jack to the campaign headquarters, Jack asked his brother to stop the car. An elderly woman was making her way back to her home, and Jack decided he would shake just one more hand.

"I'm Jack Kennedy, and I'm running for the Senate," Jack said one final time, grasping the old woman's hand in his. "I sure hope you'll vote for me tomorrow."

The next day, the race was too close to call. Jack and Bobby stayed up late into the night waiting for the decision. At nearly 3:00 in the morning, it looked as if Lodge had won, and an exhausted and disappointed Jack went to sleep. Bobby, however, stayed up all night, nervously pacing by the telephone. Finally, at 7:00 the next morning, the final numbers were in. Jack had won by nearly 3 percent of the vote.

Lodge, of course, had hoped to win, but he knew he had met his match in Jack Kennedy. In the end, it had been Kennedy's likability, even to his opponent, that had been the deciding factor.

"So often in a campaign, you look for a man's faults and campaign on them," Lodge later said. "Well, in Jack's case, you didn't do that."

During the last year of the Senate campaign, one of Jack's friends threw a dinner party at which he particularly wanted Jack to meet a young woman named Jacqueline. The friend kept forcing the two together, seating them next to each other on the sofa, reintroducing them, and drawing them into the same conversation. Finally, when they were seated directly across from each other at the dinner table, Jack took the hint.

"I leaned across the asparagus and asked her for a date," Jack later recalled.

Jacqueline (or "Jackie," as the Kennedy family insisted on calling her) Bouvier was quite unlike any of the other women Jack had been dating. Until Jack met Jackie, he had been looking only for fun, for women who were attractive and enjoyed parties. The last thing he wanted was a serious relationship. That all changed.

Jackie Bouvier was well educated at universities in both the United States and France. She was fluent in French and cultured from her travels around the world. When she met Jack, she was working as the inquiring photographer for the *Washington Times-Herald*. To top it off, she was unusually beautiful. Although she was twelve years younger than Jack, that didn't seem to bother either one of them. During their two years of dating, they were often apart as Jack traveled and campaigned, but that didn't strain their connection. There was a very private and solitary side to Jackie, as there was to Jack; she didn't mind time alone.

Jack Kennedy had acquired quite a reputation for being, as *The Saturday Evening Post* once described him, "the most eligible bachelor in the country," and in many ways, Jack was in no hurry to see his dating days come to an end. Still, Jackie fascinated him as no other woman had. Friends often remarked that when Jackie walked into the room, Jack's eyes never left her. Furthermore, Joseph Kennedy had repeatedly suggested that, at 35, Jack should be married. Joseph had already taken to wearing a necktie with the ambitious announcement, "Kennedy for President" written on it, and he often reminded his son that dating a lot of different women didn't look particularly presidential.

As for Jackie, she was equally fascinated by Jack, but, at first, she was not exactly drawn to the Kennedy family. In spite of all their money, the Kennedys could be a bit insecure about their status. They saw Jackie as rich, cultured, and of French heritage. Her background was similar to that of some of the people who, in the past, had snubbed the Kennedys for being Irish. Essentially, particularly to the Kennedy women, Jackie was a threat.

When the Kennedy girls first met Jackie, they whispered behind her back about her being overdressed. They snickered at how she pronounced "Jacqueline" with a French accent, and, almost instantly, began calling her "Jackie," both for ease and because it seemed to annoy her.

Bobby's wife, Ethel, a Kennedy through marriage, may have been worried that this beautiful young woman, who might also become a Kennedy through marriage, would overshadow her. When Jackie, desperate to make polite conversation, mentioned that years earlier she had hoped to become a ballet dancer, Ethel looked at Jackie's fairly large feet and rolled her eyes. "With those feet of yours?" Ethel laughed. "You'd be better off going into soccer, kid."

However, in the end, it was Joseph Kennedy's blessing that ensured the rest of the family's acceptance of Jackie. Aside from genuinely liking Jackie, Joseph recognized that she would add a touch of class to the Kennedy name. And Joseph couldn't help but think that Jackie would make the perfect First Lady.

CHAPTER 6

"I've known a lot of attractive women in my lifetime," Jack Kennedy would later say to a friend, "but of all of them there was only one I could have married—and I married her."

Jack and Jackie were married on September 12, 1953, and the wedding was one of the major social events of the year. Nationwide, newspapers wrote about it, and in Newport, Rhode Island, where the wedding took place, 3,000 people stormed through police barriers to get a glimpse of the couple leaving the church.

While honeymooning in Mexico, Jack sent a telegram to his parents: "Jackie is enshrined forever in my heart. Thanks Mom and Dad for making me worthy of her."

However, newlywed life was not always easy, particularly for Jackie. As "enshrined" as Jackie may have been in Jack's heart, he continued his old ways of pursuing and dating other women. Although Jackie was stunned by this at first, she slowly came to see it as typical behavior for a man like Jack.

"I don't think there are many men who are faithful to their wives," she once observed. "Men are such a combination of good and evil."

Kennedy's unfaithfulness would continue for the rest of his life—through his time in the Senate and even into his presidency. In today's society, where the personal lives of famous people and politicians are made known to the entire world, it may seem strange that Kennedy's affairs didn't draw more attention. However, at that time, the personal mistakes of powerful men were generally kept quiet. Men who had affairs were often excused—or even admired.

"Jack was so disciplined in so many ways," one friend would say later, trying to justify Kennedy's behavior. "Discipline was the secret of his success. But when it came to women, he was just a different person."

Some people felt that the ongoing behavior of this "different person" was Jack's one outlet from such a disciplined life and that he deserved it. Obviously, Jackie did not feel that way.

Eventually, Jackie would adjust as well as she could both to her husband's lifestyle and to the constant pressures associated with being the wife of a very famous senator. However, it would take some time. After about a year of married life, an interviewer asked Jackie Kennedy what her theories were for having a successful marriage. Jackie just shook her head and frowned. "I can't say I have any yet," she responded quietly.

One of the first issues Kennedy had to face as a senator was how to deal with Senator Joseph McCarthy and what came to be known as "McCarthyism." Wisconsin's Senator McCarthy had, like Kennedy, long been in favor of fighting the spread of Communism. At first, people admired just how focused and determined McCarthy was in digging up secret supporters of Communism, or the "Red Menace," as it was called, in the United States. After all, many people reasoned, if we could get rid of homegrown Communists, we'd be a lot safer from the growing international threat of the Red Menace.

McCarthy seemed to be able to uncover Communists everywhere: colleges, steel mills, movie studios, publishing companies, and even the State Department. Before long, people were being accused of being Communists for the flimsiest of reasons: reading a book about the Soviet Union, having lunch with someone who had recently traveled to China, or simply talking about Communism with a friend. Another of McCarthy's favorite tactics was to ask those he suspected of Communism to give the names of Communists in the United States. If a suspect gave no names (generally because no one they knew, including themselves, was involved in Communism), McCarthy labeled them "guilty."

Those who were accused were often placed on what were known as "blacklists." Once on those lists, a person could be fired from his or her job and could be refused employment anywhere else. McCarthy's obsession was ruining the lives of many innocent people.

Some began comparing McCarthy's actions to the Salem Witch Trials. In Salem, Massachusetts, in 1692, wild accusations had begun circulating about certain townspeople being witches. Although this may sound ridiculous to us today, many colonists in 1692 feared evil and witchcraft as much as Americans in the 1950s feared Communism. Before the hysteria calmed, twenty people in and around Salem were killed for being witches. Several others accused of being witches died in prison.

In the fall of 1953, McCarthy finally went too far. He accused the United States Army of hiding Communists. President Eisenhower was so furious that he refused to speak to the press about it. "I won't get into the gutter with that guy," Eisenhower said angrily. As a result, the Senate was faced with the task of deciding what to do with McCarthy.

After much debate and disagreement, the Senate finally decided to vote on a proposal to censure (formally show disapproval of) Senator

McCarthy. This was difficult for Kennedy. McCarthy and Kennedy had worked together in the early years of the anti-Communist movement, and McCarthy had become friendly with other members of Kennedy's family. If Kennedy voted against McCarthy, people might think he was being soft on Communism. But if he voted against censure, it might look as if he approved of witch-hunt tactics.

In the end, Kennedy didn't have to decide how to vote—he never made it to the Senate on the day the vote was held.

Kennedy's back problems had continued to worsen, and by late 1954, Kennedy was in so much pain that he could barely stand upright for more than an hour at a time. Doctors told him that the operation he needed was very risky. If things didn't go very well he might never walk again; if things went badly, he might die. Although he was given only a fifty-fifty chance of surviving the operation, Jack agreed to it. He did not want to live his life being barely able to move and being in constant pain.

Some people felt that it was no coincidence that Kennedy's operation happened at the same time as the vote on McCarthy. All of the Democratic senators who were present for the vote that day voted for censure. Kennedy was possibly the senator with the most to lose if he had voted. Some believed that Kennedy was intentionally avoiding the vote, and for this he was criticized for years to come.

Kennedy's back operation went well enough, but an infection set in afterward, and Kennedy lapsed into a coma. A priest was called and last rites were given. Joseph Kennedy, at his son's bedside as he had been so many years earlier, was fiercely optimistic.

"I know nothing can happen to him now," he said with confidence, "because I've stood by his deathbed three times, and each time I said goodbye to him, and each time he came back stronger."

Joseph was right. Slowly, Jack began to recover. It was a long process, one that kept Jack up nights with pain. But on the nights Jack couldn't sleep, he read and studied. He had become interested in the history of past senators who had stood by their beliefs—he wondered whether their firmness had damaged their popularity. Jack had come to a point in his career where he realized that some of the decisions he would make and some of the votes he would cast might make some people dislike him. Perhaps, at times, his decisions would make *most* people dislike him. That was the nature of politics. By studying the difficult choices other senators had made, Jack was reassured. He found that political integrity was more important than political popularity.

Some people were quick to suggest that Kennedy's interest in this particular subject was hardly random—they thought his interest was directly related to what they saw as his fear of voting for or against McCarthy. They believed that Kennedy's own guilt about avoiding the vote had led him to study senators who had been braver.

Regardless of Kennedy's reasons for his newfound interest, this period of recovery and study led Kennedy to write *Profiles in Courage*. In this book, Kennedy presented eight past senators who had risked their political careers by standing up for what they believed in.

"This is a book about that most admirable of human virtues—courage," Kennedy began. *Profiles* was instantly popular and became a national bestseller. However, as with his first book, there were those who did not believe that Kennedy had actually written it. How, they wondered, could someone recovering from surgery while working full-time as a freshman senator possibly have time to write such a good book? Kennedy was irritated by the accusations and flatly denied that anyone had written the book for him. However, to this day, many people still believe that *Profiles in Courage* was written in part by Kennedy's speechwriter, Theodore Sorensen.

In spite of the arguments over the author, Americans loved *Profiles in Courage*. The book was a reminder that, regardless of senators like Joseph McCarthy, there were good, honest politicians who were brave enough to do the right thing. One year later, Kennedy's book was awarded the Pulitzer Prize, one of the highest honors given to literature.

"I think he just wanted to put his foot in the water and see how cold it was, but he hadn't made up his mind to swim."

This was Bobby Kennedy's description of Jack's feelings when he was presented with the possibility of being chosen as the running mate for presidential nominee Adlai Stevenson in 1956. To go from freshman senator to vice president of the United States would be a huge leap—possibly into very cold water. Joseph Kennedy wasted no time informing his son that he would be "an idiot" to jump into such deep politics at such an early point in his career. But Jack could not resist the challenge. After all, his father had raised him to believe he should always strive for the top and should always win. Why should that change now?

Boosting Kennedy's confidence was the speech he had given at the Democratic National Convention earlier in the week. Kennedy had been chosen to give the convention's opening speech. In addition to being a great honor, speaking to the convention gave the young senator a lot of exposure. In 1956, television was relatively new, and this was the first time many people had seen a national political convention. Many viewers did not expect to see a politician who was young, handsome and (finally, after years of practice) a dynamic speaker.

"Kennedy came before the convention tonight as a movie star," wrote *The New York Times.* And viewers nationwide were in agreement. Those who thought of politicians as stuffy old men who gave dull speeches were intrigued. Suddenly, all across the country, people wanted to know more about John F. Kennedy. Kennedy felt the momentum and thought he might have a chance at being the nation's next vice president. Although his father was furious, Jack decided to jump in—only to realize too late that he was in over his head.

"I feel like the Indian who had a lot of arrows stuck in him. . . . It only hurts when I laugh," Kennedy told a friend after losing the vice-presidential nomination to an older, more experienced senator, Estes Kefauver.

Although he lost the nomination, Jack had come out a winner in other ways. He had gained widespread recognition, and he had charmed a nation. "Don't feel sorry for young Jack Kennedy," the *Boston Herald* advised. "Despite his defeat, he probably rates as the one real victor of the entire convention."

The *Boston Herald* was right. Stevenson lost to Eisenhower in a landslide election. And, somehow, Jack's experience of taking control of his career and making his own decision, good or bad, seemed to chase away the ever-present shadow of his brother Joe. The press often noted that Jack Kennedy was forever attempting to fulfill the dreams his father had once had for Joe Jr. But now, when a reporter asked Kennedy how Joe Jr. might have fared in this same election, Kennedy thought for a moment.

"Joe was the star of our family. He did everything better than the rest of us," Kennedy said. "Unlike me, he wouldn't have been beaten. Joe would have won the nomination."

Then Kennedy grinned. "And then he and Stevenson would have been beaten by Eisenhower, and today Joe's political career would be in a shambles and he would be trying to pick up the pieces."

The shadow of Joe Jr. had finally disappeared.

Immediately following the convention, Kennedy decided that he needed some time away. Leaving a pregnant Jackie with her mother in Rhode Island, Kennedy took off for some time on Teddy's yacht, sailing along the coast of Italy. Because Jack was fifteen years older than Teddy, he felt that he didn't really know his youngest brother. This seemed like the perfect opportunity for a little bonding.

With her husband 6,000 miles away, Jackie Kennedy was nervous and worried about her pregnancy. The previous year she had suffered a miscarriage, and now she feared the same thing would happen again. Only days after Jack left on his vacation, it did. Jackie went into premature labor and gave birth to a stillborn baby girl. At her side in the hospital was Bobby Kennedy.

"You knew that if you were in trouble, he'd always be there," Jackie later commented. What Jack had discovered about his faithful brother years earlier, Jackie discovered that night.

Because he was out of the country and out on the ocean, Kennedy did not hear the bad news for three days. A strained marriage became even more strained as Jackie pointed out that she had stayed at Jack's bedside for months when he had been recovering from back surgery, only to be abandoned by him when she was pregnant. Tempers continued to flare, and before long, newspapers reported that Senator Kennedy and his wife had separated.

Joseph Kennedy took his son aside and gave him a stern lecture. A young man who was both divorced and Catholic would not stand a chance at the presidency, he told Jack.

"God is still with you and you can be President if you want to and if you work hard," Joseph said.

Kennedy was not afraid of hard work, and he *did* want to become President. It was no longer just an obligation to fulfill his father's dream—it was Jack's dream, too. Jack knew as well as his father that something would have to change; something would have to bring him and Jackie back together.

That "something" came along on November 27, 1957. Jackie gave birth to a healthy seven-pound baby girl, Caroline Kennedy. This time, Kennedy had paced nervously in the waiting room, and when Jackie was wheeled out with their daughter, Kennedy literally sprinted down the hallway to see their child and hold his wife's hand.

For forty-year-old Jack Kennedy, this child was a turning point. Perhaps having to be responsible for a helpless baby turned his focus away from his sometimes selfish behavior. Friends who had rarely seen Jack open up and had never seen him shed one tear, even at his own brother's funeral, were struck by how emotional he was over the birth of his daughter.

"His voice cracked when he called to tell the news," Jack's oldest friend, Lem Billings, recalled. "And when he showed me the baby, he looked happier than I had seen him look in a long time. With this child, he finally had a family of his own."

CHAPTER 7

Kennedy did not waste the surge of popularity that he had gained at the 1956 Democratic National Convention. Over the next two years, he crisscrossed the country, speaking in more than thirty states, trying to reach as many Americans as he could. During this time, he never specifically said that he was preparing for the 1960 presidential campaign. After all, he was an admired author, senator, and speaker; why wouldn't he be touring the United States meeting people?

After three hundred speeches and appearances, however, Kennedy's future plans were hardly a secret. As people began realizing that Kennedy was, in fact, the strongest contender for President among the Democrats, everyone seemed to want to see him. In 1957 alone, Kennedy received more than 2,500 speaking invitations.

Americans were drawn to Kennedy for a number of reasons. For one thing, he spoke honestly. While politicians often used "doubletalk" to avoid directly answering questions, Kennedy was honest and not afraid to say what he felt. And many Americans appreciated his genuine concern for those who were poor, elderly, or discriminated against in any way. Furthermore, Kennedy had a great sense of humor. He often appeared to love laughing at himself more than anything else.

After two terms of Eisenhower as President, people were eager for a different kind of leader. In many ways, the 1950s had been a rather "grey" decade, as the United States craved security and comfort following the end of World War II. But now, as the 1960s approached, Americans wanted a little more excitement and a little more color. Kennedy's eyes twinkled as he told a joke about himself, and his voice rose in righteous anger when he spoke about poverty. He was, simply, the right personality at the right time.

Some Republicans, and even some Democrats who were not fans of Kennedy, tried to portray the young political star as all fluff and no substance. "All he has to do is smile and sign autographs, and he'll get votes," one Republican said with a little irritation. "He's the 'movie star' candidate."

While Kennedy's good looks and charisma certainly didn't hurt, he also had intelligence and experience. Now in his second term in the Senate (having beaten his opponent by a landslide in 1958), Kennedy had served on the Senate Foreign

Relations Committee and could match or surpass any politician's knowledge of foreign affairs. Along with his brother Bobby, who was now a lawyer, Kennedy had also worked on a committee that investigated criminal activity in labor unions. Bobby and Jack had taken on Jimmy Hoffa, the powerful president of the Teamsters Union, and though Hoffa was cleared of criminal charges, many Americans respected the Kennedy brothers' courage. Some of the investigation hearings were broadcast on television, and before long, both Jack and Bobby were recognized nearly everywhere they went. By early 1959, Kennedy's campaign for the presidency was beginning in earnest.

"Do you think a forty-two-year-old man can meet the demands made on a President?" an audience member asked Kennedy at a speech in Arizona. Kennedy had been asked that same kind of question again and again. Many people thought that Kennedy was too young to be the leader of the most powerful nation in the world.

Kennedy smiled, thinking that if he were elected, he would be a year older in 1960. "I don't know about a forty-two-year-old man, but I think a forty-three-year-old can," he replied with his trademark grin.

"Of course he's too young!" Kennedy's father would also joke. "But I'm 72, and I want to be around to enjoy it."

There was not much Kennedy could do about the issue of age, other than make light of it and try to convince voters that regardless of his youth, he was qualified. Kennedy realized that if some voters still believed that no man under the age of 55 should be elected President, he probably wouldn't change their minds. Age was not an issue that he could get too worked up over.

On the other hand, Kennedy spent a lot of time and energy thinking about and defending the issue of his religion. No Catholic had ever been elected President, and some Americans worried that if Kennedy became President, he would take his orders from the pope in Rome. After all, Catholics considered the pope to be their leader; why would Kennedy be any different? Again and again, Kennedy responded to people who believed the pope would be running the United States if a Catholic candidate became President.

"I do not speak for my church on public matters," Kennedy explained matter-of-factly, "and the church does not speak for me."

Still, across the country, voters stood up at meetings and asked, "Do you think a Catholic should become President?"

Once, in reply to this question from a student in Oregon, Kennedy explained that years earlier when he had entered the Navy, he had taken an oath to serve his country faithfully and with loyalty. He had taken the same oath as a congressman and then as a senator. He would take it again if elected President.

"If I was qualified to serve my country in those other capacities, I am qualified to serve it as President," Kennedy said. "No one asked my brother Joe if he had divided loyalties when he volunteered and died for his country."

The audience in Oregon cheered this response. And, little by little, so did most Americans.

On January 2, 1960, Kennedy officially declared himself a candidate for the presidency.

"I feel like a corner grocer competing with a chain store!"

Hubert Humphrey, Kennedy's strongest competition during the Democratic primary elections, had, like other candidates in past races against Kennedy, come up against what some people referred to as the "Kennedy machine." Once again, the entire family pitched in to help Jack Kennedy win the primaries, and, as Humphrey said, it made him feel like a small store going up against a huge chain store.

Kennedy, an obvious favorite in the New England states, won 85 percent of the vote in the New Hampshire primary, where he was the only serious candidate. Humphrey, a senator from Minnesota, hoped to do well in the Wisconsin primary, since Wisconsin was right next to Humphrey's own state and many of the Wisconsin voters knew him.

Then came the Kennedys. Rose and her daughters again went about setting up afternoon teas and house parties. Bobby Kennedy, working again as campaign manager, preceded his brother by visiting factories, schools, unions, and even restaurants where farmers gathered to drink coffee. Bobby would sit down and talk with people about Jack, creating curiosity about the older brother before he even arrived in the small towns to speak.

But perhaps most memorable was the new addition to the Kennedy machine. Jackie had just learned that she was pregnant again, but she made the trip to Wisconsin in the middle of a very cold winter to campaign for her husband. Everywhere Jackie went, record crowds came out to see her, even if she only waved and smiled.

"As usual, Jackie's drawing more people than I am," an amused Kennedy told a reporter.

Once, Jackie went into a Wisconsin supermarket and asked the manager if she could talk about her husband over the store's loudspeaker. The stunned manager could only nod, his mouth hanging open in awe.

"Please just keep on with your shopping while I tell you about my husband, John F. Kennedy," Jackie said quietly into the microphone. As she went on to talk about Kennedy's years in

Congress, "You could have heard a pin drop," one shopper recalled.

However, as helpful as the entire Kennedy family may have been, it was Jack Kennedy himself who ultimately won over voters. At first, Wisconsinites were skeptical. What did this rich senator from New England know about the hardships of farmers in the Midwest? How could a man who flew around in his own private jet have anything in common with the middle-class workingman? In some of the smallest towns, people had never even heard of Kennedy. Once, when Kennedy shook a man's hand and told him he was running for President, the man stared back blankly and asked, "President of what?"

In time, however, Jack's speeches drew bigger crowds, and people began to realize that Kennedy was a man who genuinely and specifically cared about the working class, the farmer, and the small business owner. To everyone's surprise, Kennedy actually knew a great deal about the very problems that people in Wisconsin faced. In the end, Kennedy beat Humphrey by more than 100,000 votes. This same pattern followed in West Virginia, another state that Humphrey had hoped to win. Again, no one had expected the son of a millionaire to know so much about the troubles of the rural coal miner, but Kennedy did. After Humphrey lost in West Virginia, he dropped out of the race altogether.

There were other strong Democrats who wanted to be their party's choice for President, including Lyndon Johnson. However, none of the candidates seemed to be a match for Kennedy's knowledge, hard work, and charisma. In mid-July of 1960, thousands of Democrats gathered in Los Angeles for the Democratic National Convention. In those days, the nomination was decided at the convention by the votes of representatives from every state (known as "delegates"). As a result, it was a wild scene, with supporters of the various candidates trying to out-cheer and outdo one another. Johnson's campaign workers handed out bright flowers with "Vote for Johnson" pins in them. Kennedy's workers handed out tie clasps shaped like Kennedy's old war boat, *PT-109*.

The number of delegate votes needed was 761. When Kennedy needed only eleven more votes to win the nomination and Wyoming pledged ten of its fifteen votes to Kennedy, Teddy, Jack's youngest brother, went bounding across the convention hall toward the Wyoming delegates waving his arms and shouting, "Ten votes won't do it! But eleven will!"

"Then let 'em all go!" the Wyoming chairman called to his delegates.

And with that, John F. Kennedy became the Democratic nominee for President of the United States in 1960.

"We stand at the edge of a New Frontier—the frontier of unfulfilled hopes and dreams, a frontier of unknown opportunities and beliefs in peril. Beyond that frontier are uncharted areas of science and space, unsolved problems of peace and war, unconquered problems of ignorance and prejudice, unanswered questions of poverty and surplus."

Kennedy spoke these words in his acceptance speech at the Democratic National Convention. At first, Kennedy and his speechwriter had created the slogan "New Frontier" simply because they thought it sounded optimistic. They thought that perhaps it would inspire people, especially young people, to vote for Kennedy, a young candidate who represented something new and exciting. However, the things Kennedy described as symbolic of a new era—exploring space, dealing with lingering problems of war, overcoming prejudice—would become the very things his presidency would be remembered for.

For his running mate, Kennedy chose one of the other men who had hoped to get the presidential nomination: Lyndon Baines Johnson, nicknamed "LBJ" for his initials. Many people, including Bobby Kennedy, thought this was a very bad choice. Johnson was older and more conservative. In 1960, the civil rights movement was gaining momentum, and many Kennedy supporters were worried that Johnson, a southerner, would be against equal rights for black Americans.

On a more personal note, Johnson had frequently verbally attacked both Kennedy and his family during the primaries. "Jack was out kissing babies while I was passing bills!" Johnson had once commented, referring to Jack's many absences from the Senate. And about Kennedy's wealth, Johnson said, "I haven't had everything given to me. Whatever I have . . . is because of whatever energy and talent I have."

Still, when Kennedy won the presidential nomination, Johnson graciously sent him a telegram that simply read: "LBJ now means Let's Back Jack."

Kennedy stood by his decision. In Johnson he saw a tireless campaigner and an honest man who stood by his beliefs. To Kennedy, the fact that Johnson was a southerner was a bonus. Kennedy had worried about getting the support of those in the South, but now he hoped that, with a Texan as his running mate, things would be different. As for Johnson, he was clearly thrilled to be chosen.

"I will go wherever John Kennedy wants me to go, because we both want America to follow the same road."

And it was yet another new road that Kennedy was about to embark upon. At the end of his acceptance speech, Kennedy acknowledged this by saying, "Now begins another long journey. . . . Give me your help. Give me your hand, your voice, and your vote."

Only one week later, the Republicans held their convention to choose their candidate. However, there was only one choice. The leading candidate was so strong that all others had dropped out of the race. He had served as Eisenhower's vice president, and he was well known and well liked by Americans. His name was Richard Nixon.

Even before Kennedy had been nominated, Nixon had begun pointing out what he considered to be Kennedy's weaknesses. Perhaps Kennedy thought his greatest strengths lay in his international experience. Nixon laughed at this idea. Tension was continuing to build between the United States and the Soviet Union over both nuclear arms and Communism. The Soviet leader, Nikita Khrushchev, was a gruff man who was known to interrupt other leaders just so he could insult them and laugh. Nixon had traveled to the Soviet Union to meet with Khrushchev, and had seen firsthand what kind of man he was. Nixon felt he had held his own with the Soviet leader, even when Khrushchev had tried to pick a fight.

"And Kennedy is the kind of man Mr. Khrushchev will make mincemeat of," Nixon told Americans. Nixon was well aware of the United States' growing fear of Soviet power. He felt it could only help his campaign to present his opponent as a weak leader. "Naïve" and "inexperienced" were two words Nixon used a lot when describing Kennedy.

Meanwhile, Kennedy was more interested in reaching voters all across the country than in bickering with Nixon. In ten weeks, he would travel 78,654 miles back and forth and up and down across the United States. He would shake hundreds of thousands of hands and work eighteen hours a day.

"Let's get this country moving again!" was a phrase Kennedy used often in speeches. His energy and desire to revitalize the United States attracted record numbers of young people. His concern for equal rights brought out crowds of black people who were already beginning to see Kennedy as something of a hero.

Still, Kennedy lagged behind in the polls. Nixon was only four years older than Kennedy, but many Americans still viewed him as the older, wiser candidate. Then, about six weeks before the election, all three television networks asked Nixon and Kennedy to hold a series of live televised debates. The popularity of television had exploded, and now nearly 90 percent of homes in the United States had a television set. This debate could make or break the presidential candidates.

Kennedy immediately agreed to the debates. After all, Nixon had spent a lot of energy putting him down. This would be Kennedy's opportunity to prove and defend himself. Nixon's advisers, on the other hand, warned him not to debate Kennedy. Television had made Kennedy a star— he looked good on camera and had a natural and relaxed sense of how to use television to his benefit. Nixon did not.

However, Nixon scoffed at those who told him not to debate. He had an immense amount of public speaking experience. As vice president, he had had to "debate" leaders and politicians from around the world. Why, he had even been on his high school and college debate teams!

What could possibly go wrong?

CHAPTER 8

"Television is good to Kennedy," wrote one newspaper after the first debate. "It makes Kennedy look forceful. It makes Nixon look guilty."

"Overnight," another reporter wrote, "supporters seethed with enthusiasm and multiplied in numbers, as if the sight of Kennedy on TV . . . had given him a 'star quality' reserved only for television and movie idols."

Prior to the first debate on September 26, 1960, the press had made much of the differences between Kennedy's and Nixon's speaking styles. Nixon loved to smile broadly, wave at the crowd, and point at people before speaking. He would often introduce his wife, Pat, by hugging her and booming, "Now I ask you, isn't she wonderful?" Kennedy, on the other hand, was very direct and got right to his speech without a lot of crowd-pleasing tactics. Although Jackie had accompanied Kennedy to a few states during the primary elections, he was reluctant to pull her into the presidential campaign and parade her around.

Furthermore, as one reporter noted, "Kennedy had a marvelous sense of humor; Nixon, almost none at all." Kennedy loved nothing more than poking fun at himself. In particular, Kennedy was amused when Americans teased him about his strong Boston accent. Once in Iowa, Kennedy asked, "What is the biggest problem facing the American farmer?" pronouncing "farmer" as "fahma." In the two-second pause before Kennedy continued, someone in the audience shouted out, "He's stahving!" Out of politeness, few people laughed, but Kennedy burst into such uncontrollable laughter that soon the entire audience laughed along with him.

Nixon, however, was quite serious, rarely willing to joke about his own mistakes or personality quirks. For all his enthusiasm and wide smiles, he was not exactly comfortable having anyone point out what was unusual or funny about him. Nixon wanted to be liked by everyone, and he seemed to be afraid that he might lose votes if he admitted to any laughable traits. He was unable to see that this very lack of humor may, in fact, have lost him votes.

As the first debate approached, people considered the styles of these two very different candidates. Many people felt that Nixon's smooth manner and experience would sweep all four debates. Others argued that Kennedy's more "real" behavior would help him to win. The day before the first debate, polls showed that Americans were exactly evenly split in their support for the two candidates.

That would change after the first debate on September 26.

Nixon may have been at ease in front of campaign crowds on the road, but he was very nervous before the first debate on television. He paced backstage, sweating and worrying. Because of his pale complexion, producers asked if he'd like some makeup. He waved them away in irritation. Of course he was not going to wear makeup!

As the two men took their places at their podiums, seventy million Americans tuned in to watch. From the start, Kennedy appeared calm and thoughtful while Nixon seemed distracted and jittery. When Nixon responded to a question, he turned to face Kennedy, a technique he had learned on his old debate teams. However, when Kennedy answered, he looked directly into the television cameras. He knew that he was answering the questions for Americans at home, not for his opponent.

Making matters worse, Nixon had spent the previous two weeks in the hospital with an infected knee. He had lost about twenty pounds, and the weight loss, along with his pale complexion and gray suit, made him appear washed out and weak—even sick. Kennedy's suntan and dark suit gave him an appearance of strength and good health. The contrast was so drastic that Nixon's press secretary rushed to send out a statement that announced, "Vice President Nixon is in excellent health and looks good in person."

But the difference between the two candidates went beyond appearances. Kennedy's responses were thoughtfully delivered and were spoken with command. Nixon seemed confused at times, defensive at other times, and tense the entire time. More than once, he backed down by saying "No comment" rather than engaging in debate with Kennedy. Kennedy never let up, arguing decisively and proving all his points.

When the debate was over, Bobby Kennedy summed it up: "Nixon had built up the idea that he was the only one who could stand up to Khrushchev, that a man of maturity was needed. The first debate indicated that not only could John Kennedy stand up to Nixon, he could better him. . . . it destroyed the whole basis of Nixon's campaign in one night."

And so it did. The following morning, polls showed that Kennedy had suddenly pulled ahead of Nixon. Nixon would never regain his momentum.

In the fall of 1960, black demonstrators throughout the South were protesting unfair laws. One of these laws kept black people from eating in the same restaurants as white people. Years earlier, civil rights leader Martin Luther King, Jr., had shared with black activists his belief in nonviolent protest. King taught that protesting peacefully, through marches, gatherings, and speeches, was always more effective than violence. Peaceful protest eventually shamed racists into doing the right thing.

As a result of King's teachings, some young black people had begun sitting at "white only" lunch counters throughout the South and refusing to move until they were either waited on or arrested. These protests became known as "sit-ins," and about half the time, the participants were hauled off to jail. On October 19, 1960, King decided to join a sit-in in Atlanta, Georgia.

King had been arrested numerous times in the past for taking part in peaceful protests, and on this morning in Atlanta, he was arrested again. Generally, King would serve a brief sentence and walk out of the jail only days later, but this time the authorities decided to teach him a lesson. Using an old traffic violation, the police claimed that King was still on probation, and now that he had been arrested again, his punishment would be much more severe. King was sentenced to four months of hard labor one hundred miles away in a dangerous penitentiary. It was not uncommon for black men to simply "disappear" from such backwoods prisons, never to be seen or heard from again.

"They're going to kill him!" came the terrified voice of Coretta King, Martin's wife, across the phone lines. When Kennedy learned of this terribly unfair sentence, he called Coretta to express his concern and to assure her that everything would be all right. Governors of three southern states had warned Kennedy not to have anything to do with King and the whole civil rights movement. They assured him that he would lose many thousands of votes in the South if he did.

Kennedy had already been criticized by King for not doing enough about civil rights. Everyone knew that Kennedy felt that black people should not suffer discrimination. Why wasn't he saying more about that in his campaign speeches? Perhaps Kennedy felt that if he kept quiet, he was more likely to win the election, and then, as President, he could do more for civil rights. If he lost the election, he would not be able to do nearly as much. In any event, although Kennedy phoned Coretta, he refused to get involved in the matter any more deeply.

Bobby Kennedy, however, was so angry about how King was being treated that he felt he had to do something about it.

"It was disgraceful," Bobby later said. "It just burned me up. . . . the more I thought about the injustice of it . . . sentencing a citizen to four months of hard labor for a minor traffic offense."

Bobby Kennedy called the judge who had sentenced King and made it quite clear how unfair it was (not to mention illegal) to treat King in this manner. Within forty-eight hours, King was released.

When word spread about what had taken place, blacks throughout the South were grateful to the Kennedy brothers. Some who had been undecided, or who had thought that neither Nixon nor Kennedy would do much for them, were now throwing their support toward Kennedy. King's own father, who had previously announced that he would never vote for a Catholic, now changed his mind.

"If I had a suitcase of votes," King's father shouted to his very large church congregation the following Sunday, "I'd take them to Mr. Kennedy and dump them in his lap!"

Although Kennedy may have lost some votes from whites in the South, he gained even more votes from grateful black voters.

As Election Day grew closer, the polls showed that Nixon and Kennedy were still quite close, even though Kennedy maintained his slight lead. Anything could happen. For many Americans, there were two major issues that weighed heavily on their minds. One was the growing demand for civil rights, and the other was what was known as the "Cold War."

The "Cold War" was the name given to the ongoing tension between the United States and the Soviet Union. Both countries possessed nuclear weapons, and though there had been no direct threats against the United States, Americans worried that the Communist Soviets would use their weapons to take over the country. As a result, the United States continued to build up its nuclear weapons in order to match the Soviet stockpile. Then, as soon as the U.S. weapon stockpile seemed to be larger than theirs, the Soviets would rush to build even more weapons. This was known as the "arms race."

Furthermore, the Soviets seemed to be moving ahead more quickly than the United States in areas of technology and space travel. Both the United States and the Soviet Union had launched satellites that orbited the earth. However, the Soviet Union had launched theirs first. One of the Soviets' space probes had hit the surface of the moon, and one of their satellites had carried a dog that returned safely to earth. The United States' NASA program had yet to match these feats, and some Americans were nervous that Soviet superiority in space exploration would develop into superiority in warfare.

It was, indeed, time for a New Frontier, and Kennedy was well aware that the candidate who seemed the best prepared to lead Americans into these new realms would be the candidate who would win on November 8.

Finally, it was Election Day—and what a long day it would turn out to be. Jack and Jackie walked to a branch of the Boston Public Library and, amid dozens of photographers, cast their votes. Then they headed to Hyannis Port, Massachusetts, a coastal area where Jack and many of his brothers and sisters had vacation homes. In fact, so many of the Kennedys gathered there for holidays and time off that the area became known as the "Kennedy Compound."

The Kennedy family sat around Bobby's living room for most of the day, watching the news and the election results. Thirty telephones and four wire-service machines had been set up so that the Kennedys could receive the very latest news from polls all across the country. Midway through the day, the CBS news computer predicted that Nixon was going to win by a shocking 100 to 1 margin.

"That computer is nuts," Kennedy said in a phone call to CBS. When, only forty-five minutes later, the same computer predicted that Kennedy would win with 51 percent of the vote, CBS had to agree that their computer was confused. The confusion continued until 3:00 in the morning, when Kennedy threw his hands in the air in frustration and announced that he was going to bed.

When Kennedy awoke the next morning, he thought he heard voices and cars outside his home. He peered out the window and saw Secret Service agents surrounding the entire six-acre Kennedy Compound. That was a very good sign. Then when Kennedy walked downstairs for breakfast, three-year-old Caroline came running up to her father with a wide smile.

"Good morning, Mr. President," she said with a giggle.

Kennedy had won by an amazingly narrow margin: one-tenth of one percent. None of the computers had predicted that.

Kennedy scooped up his daughter and took her for a celebratory piggyback ride along the beach. When he returned, the press had gathered, waiting for some kind of announcement from the new President. After making a few remarks and reading the congratulatory telegram from Nixon, Kennedy looked around the room for a moment and smiled.

"So now my wife and I prepare for a new administration," he concluded, "and for a new baby."

Only two and a half weeks later, the Kennedys' second child, John F. Kennedy, Jr., was born.

Inauguration Day, January 20, 1961, was freezing cold in Washington, D.C., but Kennedy refused to wear an overcoat or a hat. He wanted to present an image of youth and strength as he addressed the nation. For the singing of the national anthem, Kennedy had chosen Marian Anderson, an African American. This had never been done before, but Kennedy wanted to make it clear that he would be reaching out to help give blacks equal opportunities. And sitting on the podium near the new President was a famous poet, Robert Frost. Poets weren't usually included in inaugural events, but Kennedy wanted the nation to see that he was going to be a President who would support the arts.

Kennedy intended to be a new kind of President for a new generation.

While Kennedy's inaugural address was one of the shortest ever given, it remains one of the most memorable. Instead of throwing out promises or giving a pep talk, Kennedy offered a challenge. He pointed out that there would be no easy solutions to the problems Americans faced, but he assured the nation that hard work and sacrifice would always lead the United States in the right direction.

"Let every nation know . . . that we shall pay any price, bear any burden, meet any hardship, support any friend, oppose any foe, to assure the survival and success of liberty," Kennedy continued. "All this will not be finished in the first one hundred days. Nor will it be finished in the first one thousand days . . . nor even perhaps in our lifetime on this planet. But let us begin."

Near the end of his speech Kennedy issued his now famous call to Americans to begin the work that lay ahead: "And so, my fellow Americans: ask not what your country can do for you—ask what you can do for your country."

CHAPTER 9

"I thought this part of being President was going to be fun," Kennedy said to his brother Bobby as he frowned at the very long list of jobs that he was going to have to fill in the Cabinet, White House, and numerous agencies. He would need to choose just the right people in order for things to run smoothly.

"People, people, people!" Kennedy exclaimed, pretending to pull his hair out. "I don't know any people. I only know voters. How am I going to fill twelve hundred jobs?"

In time, however, Kennedy would fill the positions. In fact, assigning the Cabinet jobs was not that difficult for Kennedy. He had already been thinking about it, and he was determined to choose the men for these jobs (unfortunately, at that time women were not considered) based upon their knowledge and integrity—not upon whether they were Democrat or Republican. Both the secretary of defense and the secretary of the treasury were Republicans.

The one Cabinet position that Kennedy was reluctant to announce was that of attorney general. Kennedy knew that the position required an excellent lawyer, someone who was passionate about the legal system, and someone Kennedy could trust. Kennedy had just the man in mind: his brother Bobby. Bobby was not easy to convince. It wasn't that he didn't want the job. Bobby was worried about the press making a big deal out of Kennedy hiring his own little brother. He dreaded the negative response the announcement would undoubtedly bring.

Kennedy tried to joke about it, saying, "I'll make the announcement around 2:00 a.m. when no one's around, and then I'll stick my head out and whisper, 'It's Bobby.'"

Eventually, Bobby accepted the position, but, as he had feared, the press pounced on Kennedy, asking whether he thought it was a bad idea to have family members taking over Cabinet positions. Bobby stood to the side looking flustered and a bit guilty. Kennedy, however, remained cool, replying dryly that he did not intend to hire his entire family, just his brother.

"Plus," Kennedy added with a playful grin, "I see no reason why Bobby shouldn't get a little experience before he goes out to practice law."

The members of the press laughed at Kennedy's joke and dropped the subject. Kennedy's humor would continue to be a valuable tool throughout his presidency. Finding just the right words to make people laugh sometimes did more to ease a tense situation than any serious words could ever do.

Once Kennedy had his Cabinet and all of his aides in place, he and his family began adjusting to life in the White House. It had been fifty years since children had lived in the White House, and now Americans could not get enough pictures and stories about Caroline and John Jr. The President's desk, a huge desk made from the wood of an 1800s British warship, was a favorite play place for both children. When they discovered that it had a "secret" panel in the front that could swing open, they began hiding behind it when their father conducted meetings in the Oval Office.

"We would hear a scratching noise behind the panel of the desk," one Cabinet member recalled, "and the President would exclaim, 'Is there a rabbit in there?'"

With those words, both Caroline and her brother would fling open the panel and dash out, giggling and falling down on the floor in fits of laughter.

At times, in the midst of a serious meeting, Kennedy would gaze out of his office windows to see his son and daughter playing in the back yard. Then, completely disregarding the meeting for just a few minutes, the President would walk to the back door of his office and clap his hands until both children came running to him. In spite of the pain in his back, Kennedy would reach down and tenderly pick up both Caroline and John Jr., holding one in each arm.

"His face was more relaxed in those moments than I had ever seen it with any adult," remembered Kennedy's friend and speechwriter, Theodore Sorensen. "No friend ever drew so close to John Kennedy, or contributed so much to his spirit and strength, as his wife, his daughter, and his son."

Kennedy had spent three years campaigning nearly nonstop. During those years, he was often bitterly sad to be away from his wife and baby daughter. Now, it seemed no one could really blame him for interrupting meetings to spend a few moments with his children. As one observer pointed out, now that Kennedy was in the White House, he was finally home.

However, as Jackie liked to remind the American public every now and then, the children were not always the angels the press made them out to be. John Jr. and his sister could be as mischievous as any children their age. At times, John Jr. insisted on being part of Cabinet meetings, walking around with an overly serious expression and shaking everyone's hands before pulling up a chair and refusing to leave. And once, when Kennedy was too tired to meet with the press that had gathered in the lobby of the White House, Caroline decided to take over for her father. When asked where her father was, Caroline just shrugged and announced, "He's sitting upstairs with his shoes and socks off not doing anything."

For Jackie Kennedy, life in the White House presented some unique opportunities. She had looked around the old mansion and decided that it needed some major updating. The very first thing on her list was to redo the White House library, making sure that it contained many of the classics that she and Jack loved. In particular, she had many volumes of great American literature placed in the library. Next, she had bookshelves built in both the children's bedrooms and in her and Jack's bedroom. Years later, Caroline Kennedy would recall how important books were in the Kennedy household. "They read to us all the time," Caroline said of her parents. "So, naturally, we learned to love books, too."

Books and bookshelves, however, were just the beginning.

"The White House belongs to the American people," Jackie explained. She felt that Americans should be proud of the home the President and his family lived in. But much of the White House's interior had little character and no history attached to it. Jackie began looking for historical furnishings, even digging around in corners of the

White House basement to find old belongings of past Presidents, such as Thomas Jefferson and James Monroe. Walls were repainted and floors refinished. Flowers and plants were strategically placed.

By the time Jackie was finished, the White House was so transformed that a televised tour through the White House was aired. More than fifty million Americans tuned in to watch. Children were particularly interested in seeing the big desk in which Caroline and John Jr. hid. And beyond the gardens, there was a barn that housed Caroline's pony, Macaroni. In the weeks that followed, Jackie Kennedy received 10,000 letters from children who were curious about people their own age living in the White House.

President Kennedy's redecorating concerns, however, were fairly limited. He was mostly just very eager to get started in his job as President. Even though the day after Kennedy's inauguration was a Saturday, and even though he had been up until 2:00 a.m. attending parties and balls, he insisted on having his aides gathered in his office at 9:00 Saturday morning. As they all settled around the meeting table, Kennedy looked at the bare walls and, excusing himself, jumped up and left the room. When he returned, his arms were full of pictures of Jackie, Caroline, and John Jr. Smiling sheepishly, he began hanging some of them.

Aside from pictures of his family, Kennedy's most treasured item in his office was a paperweight on his desk. It was an unusual-looking item—an old brown husk with what looked like a handful of words scratched on it, placed in a bronze holder. It was, in fact, the coconut Jack had used to send a message for help when he and his crew were stranded after the loss of *PT-109*. Sitting directly in front of the President on his desk, the coconut constantly reminded him of the importance of bravery, sacrifice, and service to one's country.

Two weeks before Kennedy's inauguration, the Soviet Union's Khrushchev had been publicly patting himself on the back for being, he believed, a much stronger and tougher leader than this young Jack Kennedy could ever hope to be. Khrushchev bragged that Communism was going to take over the world. He looked at poverty-stricken, undeveloped countries (called "third world countries") with a gleam in his eye. He thought that people who were too poor to help themselves would welcome any kind of help—even from a Communist country.

Khrushchev called the planned takeovers of these third world countries "wars of national liberation," and he boasted that before long, Communism would rule the entire world. Kennedy knew that the Cold War was something that Americans worried about, but more troubling to Kennedy were the vast parts of the world where people were suffering too much to know or care that a Communist takeover would not liberate them.

"Our greatest challenge," Kennedy told the American people, "is in the world beyond the Cold War."

Kennedy looked at parts of Asia, Latin America, Africa, and the Middle East where people were living lives unimaginable to most Americans, and he came up with an idea that would help those countries. Kennedy wasn't interested in sending yet another American foreign aid package—he wanted to send Americans. Years earlier, Senator Hubert Humphrey had presented the idea of a program where Americans with useful skills or knowledge would travel to poor countries and teach the people there how to help themselves and make their lives better.

However, the idea was mostly ignored. Who in his or her right mind, members of Congress had argued, would want to spend two years in poor, filthy, and often dangerous conditions— *and* do it all without pay, as a volunteer?

Kennedy had more faith in Americans. He believed that many people would actually love the opportunity to represent their country in a positive way. Some poor countries viewed the United States as non-caring and selfish, more concerned about fighting wars than about helping others. Kennedy saw this new organization as a way to combat that negative image of the U.S. as a war-loving country. He named the organization the Peace Corps and told Americans that the two-year assignments would not be easy and would not pay anything. He also said that the experience would be priceless in terms of what the volunteers could both give and get back.

Young people, particularly, were eager to travel and help others. They could not sign up fast enough. Within two years, 7,100 Americans, most under the age of 30, were serving in forty-four countries. Today, nearly half a century after Kennedy started the Peace Corps, thousands of Americans continue to volunteer and make a difference. Although Kennedy would be remembered for many accomplishments, his establishment of the Peace Corps is often considered to be one of his brightest moments.

However, barely thirty days after Kennedy created the Peace Corps, one of the darker moments of his presidency occurred.

Just ninety miles off the southeastern coast of the United States, the island of Cuba was beginning to pose a threat. In 1959, Fidel Castro had taken over Cuba after leading a revolution that had overthrown the former dictator, a man that most Cubans disliked. Although Castro had promised a democratic election so that Cubans could choose their new leader, he didn't keep that promise, and he continued to stay in charge of the small island country. While some Cubans were unhappy with this, Castro remained popular enough. He was a charismatic man with a booming laugh, and he was never seen without a Cuban cigar proudly clenched between his teeth. Castro's swagger and fierce attitude seemed to make him larger than life. Even Cubans who didn't necessarily agree with his politics were often drawn to Fidel Castro.

And now Castro had also drawn the attention and admiration of the Soviet Union's Khrushchev. Before long, Khrushchev and Castro began forming a close friendship, and pictures of the two of them laughing and hugging began to show up in newspapers around the world. Castro supported Communism and had put a Communist government in place in Cuba. In addition, he seemed more than willing to do whatever the rich and powerful Khrushchev asked of him. Once a harmless little island off the coast of Florida, Cuba had become a very real danger to the United States.

While Eisenhower had still been President, he and the Central Intelligence Agency (CIA) had worked on secret plans for disrupting Castro's life and making him appear unfit to be a leader. They thought that perhaps Cubans would throw him out of office if he seemed to be mentally or physically ill. There had been plots to sprinkle his clothing with a type of powder that would make his beard fall out. Other agents had suggested dipping his cigars in a chemical that would make him appear drunk when giving a speech. Still others supported spraying the drug LSD on the microphone in Castro's personal broadcast studio. However, in the end, the CIA and Eisenhower decided upon "executive action." This was the code name for an assassination.

During the final months of Eisenhower's presidency, the CIA botched one murder plan after another. Poison pills dropped in Castro's water glass didn't dissolve. A box of poisoned cigars disappeared along with the Cuban official who was supposed to deliver it. Hired assassins changed their minds at the last minute. Finally, the CIA decided on an entirely different tactic: an invasion of Cuba.

When Kennedy became President, 1,400 Cuban exiles (Cubans who had left Cuba because they refused to support Castro) were living in Miami, Florida, and were already training for the invasion. The exiles had told American officials that most Cubans were dissatisfied with Castro and would gladly support a strong American attack. In fact, the exiles had said that most Cubans would likely join in a revolt against Castro. These reports from the exiles encouraged the CIA to act.

The plan was for the army of exiles, known as the "Cuban Brigade," to secretly arrive on two different Cuban shores near a body of water called the Bay of Pigs. They would be followed by destroyer ships, U.S. aircraft carriers, and backup troops. The Cuban Brigade would then hide in the nearby mountains (where many Cubans lived), organize an uprising against Castro, and capture him. If any extra help was needed, the U.S. military would be waiting quietly in the hidden bay.

Kennedy inherited this plan when he became President, and he was expected to follow through on it. He was also instructed to keep the entire operation secret. In fact, just three days before the invasion began, he told the American public that the United States had no intention of attacking Cuba or Castro in any way.

Kennedy was unsure about the plan, and he had the power to refuse to carry it out, but he gave the go-ahead anyway. After all, if the invasion was a success, it would be a remarkable strike against Communism, something that would prove Kennedy was a strong and able leader. What's more, the CIA assured Kennedy that the plan was airtight, and they strongly advised him to proceed with it.

Still, on the day before the invasion, April 16, 1961, Kennedy paced the Oval Office. He reread CIA briefings and frowned. Late that afternoon, as he played a round of golf with his brother-in-law, he discussed the upcoming attack. It was scheduled to begin at midnight, only hours away. At one point, Kennedy sighed deeply and shook his head, looking first at his watch and then staring off into the distance.

"It just doesn't feel right," Kennedy admitted quietly.

CHAPTER 10

"That's not seaweed! Those are coral reefs!" a commander of one of the U.S. military ships shouted out to the navigator. Within minutes, several crews entering the Bay of Pigs struck the hard coral and had to either turn back or abandon ship. Those dark spots that the CIA had seen on radar were certainly not the harmless seaweed patches they had appeared to be.

Making matters worse, the Bay of Pigs harbor was not at all what the CIA had thought it was. To begin with, it was one of Fidel Castro's favorite fishing spots—he knew it very well. Far from being a quiet harbor inhabited only by locals, it was a brightly lit and well guarded area, complete with a radio tower. Almost the instant the ships appeared, Castro was informed of the invasion, and Cuban fighter jets and troops rushed to the Bay of Pigs. Contrary to what the CIA had believed, Cubans were more than willing to defend their country and their leader.

But most tragic of all, the 1,400 members of the Cuban Brigade found themselves trapped on the harbor's shore. The mountains where they were supposed to hide were much farther away than the CIA had thought, and the shoreline was a muddy swamp that made movement—either forward or backward—impossible. The Cuban exiles were trapped. As the men watched helplessly, their ships were fired upon and bombed by jets. Soon, Castro's forces arrived, capturing or killing all but 150 of the 1,400 members of the Cuban Brigade. The invasion had been a complete disaster.

Kennedy was horrified by what had happened. He was stunned that men whose abilities and knowledge he had trusted had been so wrong. Although his presidency was barely three months old, Kennedy was suddenly a changed man.

"He was totally different in his attitude toward everything," a close friend of Kennedy's explained. "Before the Bay of Pigs, everything was a glorious adventure, onward and upward. Afterwards it was a series of ups and downs. . . . suspicion everywhere, cautious of everything, questioning always."

Kennedy called his father for advice and comfort, but Joseph Kennedy was too angry to comfort his son, telling him that if the job was too much for him he should hand it over now to Lyndon Johnson. Joseph blamed the CIA, claiming, "I know that outfit, and I wouldn't pay them a hundred bucks a week!"

However, Kennedy was not one to shift the blame to others. "How could I have been so stupid?" he asked over and over again in the flurry of meetings that followed.

Finally, in a televised press conference, Kennedy told Americans about the secret attack on Cuba and its disastrous outcome. He took full responsibility for everything that had happened.

"There is an old saying that victory has a hundred fathers and defeat is an orphan," Kennedy said, his sad eyes void of the characteristic twinkle Americans had come to expect when they saw him speak. "I am the responsible officer of the government."

Though Kennedy had not passed along the blame, he had learned an important lesson: Never again would he blindly follow the advice of others when his own instincts directed him differently.

In the weeks that followed, Jackie recalled that she had never seen Kennedy so upset. He stayed up nights worrying about the members of the Cuban Brigade who had been taken as prisoners. He spoke again and again about the men who had been trapped and killed.

Kennedy had made a bad mistake within his first 100 days in office, but the American public could not seem to fault a man who humbly admitted his own failures. Immediately following the Bay of Pigs blunder, Kennedy's approval ratings shot up 16 percent.

"I have to show him that we can be just as tough as he is," Kennedy said of Khrushchev not long after the Bay of Pigs. "I'll have to sit down with him, and let him see who he's dealing with."

One of the first things Kennedy had done when he had become President was to contact Khrushchev and request a meeting so that, hopefully, some of the tensions of the Cold War could be relieved. Khrushchev laughed scornfully at Kennedy's invitation and ignored it. However, after the Bay of Pigs disaster, Khrushchev believed he had the upper hand and that Kennedy would give in to some of his demands.

And there was one demand in particular that the Soviet leader wanted to force on Kennedy. Since the end of World War II, the city of Berlin, in Germany, had been divided. West Berlin had been under control of the United States and its allies in Europe, while East Berlin was controlled by the Soviets. Now Khrushchev wanted all of Berlin, meaning that the entire city would be under Communist rule. Berliners resisted Communism, and for years, East Berliners had been moving to West Berlin to escape Khrushchev's rule. Now the Soviet leader thought he saw a chance to bully the United States into giving him all of Berlin. After all, Kennedy must be ashamed and vulnerable after such a crushing defeat. Quickly, Khrushchev agreed to a summit meeting (a meeting of heads of state) in Vienna, Austria.

Back in Washington, Kennedy was well aware of Khrushchev's intentions. It made the young President all the more determined to meet with the Soviet leader and show him that he was not some naïve kid that could be pushed around. More important, though, Kennedy sincerely hoped to find some middle ground, some sense of mutual understanding that would help to begin the thawing of the Cold War.

That was not to be.

While both leaders were stiffly polite to one another, no agreements were reached. Khrushchev was irritated by the idea that the Soviets were seen as being to "blame" for the spread of Communism. In his mind, the United States was a rich, spoiled country where everyone had been brainwashed into believing that their form of government was the best. Khrushchev believed that the Soviet Union had the right to be Communist, and if other countries around the world preferred Communism, that was their choice. The United States, he concluded, should mind its own business.

When pressed about Berlin, Kennedy would not back down. Khrushchev appeared frustrated and angered by Kennedy's refusal to even consider giving all of Berlin to the

Soviets. Further frustrating the Soviet leader was Kennedy's calm self-assurance. Kennedy was not easily flustered, and while Khrushchev could intimidate many important men, he could not seem to rattle this young leader. In fact, Kennedy was so at ease, he even poked a bit of fun at Khrushchev.

Once, during a break in the summit meeting, Kennedy gazed at several medals pinned to Khrushchev's jacket. "What are the medals for?" Kennedy asked through an interpreter.

"They are peace medals," Khrushchev replied proudly.

Kennedy looked at them a bit longer as a slow smile covered his face. "Well," he replied, "I hope you get to keep them."

While both men laughed at this, the end result of the Vienna Summit was no laughing matter. In fact, it seemed as if the meeting had made the Cold War a little chillier. The thought that the only two countries with nuclear weapons could not seem to get along with each other was indeed chilling.

Kennedy later said of the meeting, "I did not come away with any feeling that an understanding . . . so that we do not go over the brink . . . would be easy to reach."

How close was this "brink" that Kennedy referred to? And which country would be going over it? A little more than a year after the Vienna

Summit, John F. Kennedy feared that the brink was in sight.

"We have some big troubles," Kennedy said in a phone call to his brother Bobby on the morning of October 16, 1962. "I want you over here right away."

That morning, the President's national security adviser had interrupted Kennedy's breakfast to show him some very disturbing photographs. For some time, United States security had been keeping an eye on Cuba. Because of its ties to the Soviet Union and its short distance from the United States, Cuba was still considered a serious threat.

"What are these?" the President asked, staring at what looked like a line of long barns.

"We've confirmed that they are nuclear missile sites, sir," the security adviser said nervously.

Still in his bathrobe, Kennedy called for an emergency meeting of top advisers, officials, and close friends. The group became known as the "Executive Committee," or "ExComm" for short.

ExComm reviewed all the photos carefully, and the conclusion was devastating. Specialists estimated that there was already enough missile power in Cuba to kill nearly 100 million Americans in a matter of minutes.

Kennedy and ExComm knew that there was only one place all those nuclear weapons could have come from: the Soviet Union. At first, Khrushchev gruffly denied knowing anything about missiles and launchers in Cuba. Then when Kennedy pointed out that United States security had observed Soviet freighters unloading military weapons, Khrushchev tried to claim that those were other supplies, not weapons. However, he quickly changed his story. Yes, those were nuclear weapons, he responded icily, but they had been sent to Cuba only for defense if the United States attacked Cuba.

Kennedy and ExComm were not about to believe that.

For some time, the United States had been winning the arms race. American military already had missiles that could reach all the way to the Soviet Union, but the Soviets lagged far behind in their development of long-range missiles. That bothered Khrushchev terribly, so he had made a deal with Fidel Castro: If Castro would allow the missile sites in Cuba, right next to the United States, Khrushchev would protect Cuba from any U.S. attacks.

This had seemed to Castro like the perfect plan. Within the year, nuclear warheads were aimed at seven major U.S. cities. Now, Khrushchev thought, the United States and the Soviet Union were equally matched. The only question was who would push the nuclear button first, who would be the first to go over the brink.

This was a moment Kennedy had hoped never to see. Bobby Kennedy later recalled his brother's obvious terror in the daylong and deep-into-the-night meetings that were held as they tried to resolve this crisis: "His hand went up and covered his mouth. He opened and closed his fist. His face seemed drawn, his eyes pained, almost grey. We stared at each other across the table."

To Kennedy, the power to "push the button" was a monstrous power and one that he wished he did not have. The arms race was one he had entered by way of becoming President, and now all he wanted was for the race to end without the use of any of the nuclear arms that both countries possessed. For days, ExComm met and discussed how to handle this frightening situation. There was a great deal of disagreement. Five very different plans were considered:

1. Use political pressure to make the Soviets remove the missiles.
2. Invade Cuba.
3. Destroy the missiles with an air attack.
4. Block all ships from going to Cuba (known as a naval blockade).
5. Do nothing at all.

At first, the idea of doing nothing at all was appealing. After all, the United States also had nuclear weapons in Turkey, quite close to the Soviet

Union. Perhaps Khrushchev thought, logically, that what was fair for the U.S. was also fair for the Soviet Union. Perhaps drawing attention to the fact that Americans felt threatened by the Soviets would increase Khrushchev's feelings of strength.

However, Kennedy knew in his heart that something must be done.

"The greatest danger of all," he said, looking gravely around the table of advisers, "would be to do nothing at all."

Many of the members of ExComm, including the secretary of defense, wanted to use military force and invade Cuba immediately. They felt it was best to show that we were not afraid, and destroying the missiles and launchers would be safer than trying to negotiate with Khrushchev, a man who was not to be trusted.

Kennedy and his brother resisted the idea of invading Cuba. Kennedy worried that this would lead to World War III, a war of such terrible proportions that it might destroy the entire world. And it wasn't that Kennedy feared for his own life. There were, to his thinking, so many more important lives at stake.

"If it weren't for the children, it would be so easy to press the button!" Kennedy told a friend late one night. "Not just John and Caroline and not just the children in America, but children all over the world who will suffer and die for the decision I have to make."

As the Cuban missile crisis stretched out for more than a week, Americans became increasingly aware that something was going on. Finally, Kennedy decided upon a naval blockade, and 180 U.S. ships nearly surrounded Cuba, and bomber forces took to the air over Cuba. All ships approaching from the Soviet Union had been instructed to turn back around, but no one knew whether or not that would happen. People thought that perhaps the war would begin on the water. Around the world, all U.S. military personnel were put on high alert.

Rumors, speculation, and alarm began to spread across the country. Kennedy had wanted to spare Americans fear as long as possible, but now he knew it was time to come forward with the difficult news. On October 22, six days after seeing the pictures of the missiles, Kennedy spoke to the nation.

"Good evening my fellow citizens. This government, as promised, has maintained the closest surveillance of the Soviet military buildup on the island of Cuba," the President began. As Americans held their breath, Kennedy grimly explained that there were now missiles aimed at the United States just ninety miles off the U.S. coastline.

"It shall be the policy of this nation to regard any nuclear missile launched from Cuba against any nation in the Western Hemisphere as an attack by the Soviet Union on the United States, requiring a full retaliatory response upon the Soviet Union."

In short, both countries were on that brink that Kennedy had referred to eighteen months earlier. It was the brink of nuclear war.

Americans were terrified. Thousands rushed out and built fallout shelters, underground compartments with concrete walls perhaps two feet thick. Others made hasty plans to leave the large cities that were the targets of these missiles. Still others considered moving out of the United States altogether.

Two nights later, the members of ExComm sat around a table staring tensely at one another. They had just received a report that several Soviet vessels were moving at full speed toward the blockade. Accompanying them were armed Soviet submarines. They were showing no signs of slowing down. Now they were approaching the "point of no return"—the point where U.S. ships would be forced to fire upon them. This was the point where war would start.

None of the men gathered around the table spoke. Kennedy tried to appear calm, leaning over a pad of paper doodling. But the words he doodled gave him away: *serious . . . serious . . . submarines . . . submarines . . .* Bobby watched his older brother and later recalled that all he could think of was the death of Joe Jr. and Jack's near-death experiences. It seemed as if that thin line between life and death had never been so vivid to Bobby before.

Suddenly, a messenger burst into the quiet room. "Mr. President," he said breathlessly, "some of the Russian ships are stopping."

All the men in the room looked toward Kennedy. No one said a word. Finally, the secretary of state, one of the men who had wanted to invade Cuba rather than form a blockade, sighed with relief.

"We're eyeball to eyeball," he said quietly, "and I think the other fellow just blinked."

CHAPTER 11

Khrushchev may have ordered the Soviet ships and submarines to turn back, but the showdown between the two countries continued. Missiles and launchers were still in Cuba, and until those were removed, the tension would remain strong. Kennedy paced the Oval Office. What was Khrushchev thinking? Until Kennedy received some sort of communication from Khrushchev, he couldn't be certain that the Soviets were not simply regrouping and planning to send more ships that, this time, would crash the blockade.

"It is insane," Kennedy said in frustration as two more days went by with no word from Khrushchev, "that two men, sitting on opposite sides of the world, should be able to decide to bring an end to civilization."

Finally, on October 26, ten days into the Cuban missile crisis, Khrushchev sent a hopeful, though rather confusing, letter. It read, in part, "If you have not lost your self-control, . . . we and you ought not to pull on the ends of the rope in which you have tied the knot of war . . . let us take measures to untie that knot."

It seemed that Khrushchev wanted a truce. In addition, Khrushchev offered to have the Cuban missiles removed and shipped back to the Soviet Union. If he did this, the crisis would come to an end.

Immediately, ExComm met to write a response to Khrushchev. Everyone was eager to move forward toward peace. However, in less than twenty-four hours, Khrushchev sent another message, which contradicted his first one. Now he was demanding that the United States remove all of its missiles from Turkey before the Soviet Union removed its missiles from Cuba. Furthermore, he had sent more fighter jets to Cuba, and just that morning an American pilot had been killed when his jet had been shot down over Cuba by Soviet forces.

"Enough is enough," several members of ExComm said angrily. "There must be an immediate airstrike on Cuba followed by an invasion."

Still, Kennedy said no. He and Bobby agreed that once the United States invaded Cuba, it would mean a full-scale war with the Soviets. But now the clock was ticking.

"The noose was tightening on all of us,"

Bobby Kennedy would later write, "on Americans, on mankind."

It was, in fact, Bobby who came up with an unusual way of dealing with Khrushchev's two very different messages. Why not simply ignore the second message and respond to the first? A message was sent to Khrushchev agreeing to the initial terms: The U.S. would not invade Cuba if the Soviet Union would remove all missiles.

By 9:00 the following morning, October 28, words of agreement came from Khrushchev. Thirteen nerve-racking days later, the Cuban missile crisis had been resolved—peacefully.

The terror of those thirteen days seemed to have had a profound effect on Khrushchev. Not long afterward, he expressed his newfound admiration for Kennedy. The young President had been wise, patient, and yet tough—a rare combination. Khrushchev also pointed out several times that he was now more interested in competing with the United States in productive ways, through space travel and technology, than in ways of war. Never again, Khrushchev said, should the world come to that terrible brink. "In the next war," he said gravely, "the survivors will envy the dead."

As a result, two months later, the Soviet Union signed the first arms control agreement ever. This was a huge accomplishment for the Kennedy administration. In addition, the Limited

Nuclear Test Ban Treaty was signed, forbidding the testing of nuclear weapons anywhere except far underground.

The Cold War did not end with the signing of these agreements, but the understanding and cooperation between the Soviet Union and the United States eased a great deal of fear.

"For in the final analysis," Kennedy said as he addressed the nation in early 1963, "our most basic common link is that we all inhabit this small planet. We all breathe the same air. We all cherish our children's future. And we are all mortal."

It was Kennedy's hope, then, that Americans would rethink their attitudes and their prejudices toward Soviet people. After all, as he pointed out, we all live in this world together; we all have the same dreams and desires. That fact was becoming more and more vivid in the United States, as African Americans continued to struggle against the prejudices that many white people still carried. Early in the civil rights movement, blacks had demonstrated peacefully for simple rights: sitting at the front of a bus, eating in the same restaurant as white people, drinking from the same fountains.

However, more important rights—equal education, fair housing, and the right to vote— were still being denied to African Americans in some parts of the United States, particularly in the

South. Although there were some laws in place, these laws were often ignored, and when black people demanded their rights, violence often resulted. In 1962, when James Meredith, a black man, had enrolled as the first African American at the University of Mississippi, a mob of thousands of angry white people had blocked the entrance to the university. Many of them had waved guns and knives.

The situation in Mississippi had become so dangerous that President Kennedy had to send in 300 federal marshals and 20,000 troops. It was the biggest military action within the borders of the United States since the Civil War. Making matters worse, the governor of Mississippi supported the racist mob.

"You don't understand the situation down here!" the governor had angrily barked at Kennedy.

"What I want is to try to work this out in an amicable way," Kennedy had responded calmly.

But it would not be worked out in a friendly way. Before the protest was over, two people were dead, twenty-eight federal marshals had been shot, and 160 protestors were injured.

Kennedy was both saddened and furious. Meredith had the *legal right* to enter that university, regardless of how much it upset racists. That night, Kennedy had addressed the nation on national television.

"Americans are free . . . to disagree with the law but not to disobey it," Kennedy had said evenly. "No mob, however unruly or boisterous, is entitled to defy a court of law."

However, in 1963, the violence continued.

In Birmingham, Alabama, thousands of blacks, led by Martin Luther King, Jr., took to the streets in peaceful protest. Immediately, the local sheriff, "Bull" Connor, arrested them and packed the city jails. When teenagers and children, some as young as six years old, bravely marched in place of the jailed adults, Connor lost his temper. In a fury, he turned vicious police dogs on the children and commanded firefighters to blast the young people with powerful jets of water from their hoses, slamming them to the ground. Photographs of children in Alabama being sprayed with tear gas and beaten with clubs were seen across the Unites States and around the world.

Perhaps, in the past, Kennedy had been overly cautious not to be too outspoken about the civil rights movement. He had worried about losing the support of southern voters, and now, with the campaign for his reelection in 1964 just around the corner, getting votes was again an important priority. But it was no longer the top priority. Kennedy watched the news of the violence against blacks in Birmingham in disgust. He was, as always, particularly concerned about the welfare of children. And as Kennedy watched the news of black children being attacked, he knew he could no longer remain quiet.

On June 11, 1963, Kennedy delivered a historic address to the nation. His feelings about the civil rights movement were now perfectly clear—he and his administration would fully support it.

"Today we are committed to a worldwide struggle to promote and protect the rights of all who wish to be free," Kennedy said that evening. "When Americans are sent to Vietnam or West Berlin, we do not ask for whites only. It ought to be possible, therefore, for American students of any color to attend any public institution they select without having to be backed up by troops. It ought to be possible for American consumers of any color to receive equal service . . . without being forced to resort to demonstrations in the street.

"Not every child has an equal talent or an equal ability or an equal motivation, but [all children] should have an equal right to develop their talent and their ability and their motivation, to make something of themselves."

Around the nation, both blacks and whites cheered Kennedy's groundbreaking speech. Martin Luther King, Jr., watching the speech with other civil rights leaders, sat quietly with a small smile on his face and a tear rolling down his cheek. Immediately, King sent Kennedy a telegram telling him that his speech was "one of the most eloquent, profound, and unequivocal pleas for justice and the freedom of all men ever made by any President."

Sadly, only hours after Kennedy's speech, there was a grim reminder of just how far the country still had to go to overcome racist hatred. Civil rights activist Medgar Evers, returning home after watching the speech with other activists, was shot in the back and killed as he walked up to his front door. The murder was witnessed by Evers's two young children. Although the white man who killed Evers was twice brought to trial, each all-white jury let him go free. He would not be retried and finally imprisoned until 1990.

That long hot summer of 1963 also saw what is considered to be one of the most awe-inspiring events of the civil rights movement. On August 28, nearly a quarter of a million people of all races and from all backgrounds gathered in Washington, D.C., for what was billed as "The March on Washington for Jobs and Freedom." In his speech, Kennedy had mentioned the creation of a civil rights act, legislation that would ensure many types of equality for blacks. Leaders of the movement did not want Kennedy to forget about this.

"Let's have a peaceful demonstration in the President's own back yard," many of the leaders said. "Let's show him how important this civil rights act is to us."

At first, Kennedy had not supported the idea of a mass gathering in Washington. As hundreds of thousands of people filled the mile of the National Mall between the Lincoln Memorial and the Washington Monument, Kennedy watched the news coverage and shook his head. If the gathering became violent or got out of hand in any way, it could give people a bad impression of the civil rights movement.

However, there were no problems at all that day. Reporters marveled at how everyone just seemed happy to be there, to be part of a historic gathering for human rights. The last speaker that afternoon was Martin Luther King, Jr. As King's powerful voice grew and a hush fell over the crowd, Kennedy listened, mesmerized by King's now-legendary words:

"I have a dream that one day on the red hills of Georgia the sons of former slaves and the sons of former slave owners will be able to sit down together at the table of brotherhood. I have a dream that one day even the state of Mississippi . . . will be transformed into an oasis of freedom and justice. I have a dream that my four little children will one day live in a nation where they will not be judged by the color of their skin but by the content of their character. *I* have a dream today!"

When the march was over, Kennedy met King and shook his hand. Looking King in the eye, Kennedy said, "I have a dream today."

As the summer of 1963 turned to fall, Kennedy began looking ahead to 1964, when he would, hopefully, be elected to his second term as President. Throughout the South, many voters were now terribly angry with Kennedy. Some governors were already campaigning against Kennedy's reelection. And the Ku Klux Klan sent repeated death threats to the President. But Kennedy would not soften his stand on equal rights for all Americans.

"This issue could cost me the election," he told a friend that summer, "but we're not turning back."

Kennedy's years as President were not all about the stress of a Cold War and the often frustrating and heartbreaking fight for civil rights. Jack, along with Jackie, found the time to enjoy and promote cultural aspects of life that were important to them. During their years in the White House, the Kennedys made some big changes that caused the American public to view the President and the First Lady differently than they had in the past.

Americans had come to think of the White House simply as the place where the President lived and where important meetings took place. But now, it had turned into something of a palace where the best musicians, actors, artists, and writers often gathered with the Kennedys for dinner parties and performances. At one memorable dinner, Kennedy had invited an amazing group of Nobel Prize winners. As he looked around the table, Kennedy grinned and made a toast by saying, "I think this is the most extraordinary collection of talent, of human knowledge, that has ever been gathered at the White House—with the possible exception of when Thomas Jefferson dined alone."

The United States had often been viewed as having less culture than Europe, but now even Europeans admired the Kennedy family and the flair and fashion they gave to American politics. Britain's prime minister compared the Kennedys to a royal family. One British reporter wrote, "No matter what one thinks about JFK's politics, one must admit that the Kennedys have class."

Kennedy had managed to build a world around himself and his family that was not unlike the kingdom of Camelot he had read about and loved as a child. The glamour, style, and culture that now graced the White House led many, in fact, to think of the Kennedy era as a new

"Camelot," with Kennedy being the admired king and Jackie being his beautiful queen.

Not only were Europeans intrigued by Kennedy, many Americans were totally captivated by the President and his family. It seemed that everyone wanted to know even the smallest and most unimportant details of the Kennedys' day-to-day life. "President's Son Gets a Haircut . . ." read headlines in the typically no-nonsense *New York Times*. "John Jr. Refers to Father as 'Foo-Foo Head'!" blared a magazine headline. And the fact that Caroline had taken off her clothes to play in a fountain on the White House lawn was more pressing news than how the stock market had fared that day.

Perhaps just as important to Kennedy as recognizing the value of the arts was recognizing the importance of dreaming big dreams. Before Kennedy became President, the Soviet Union had been ahead of the United States in the space race, but Kennedy's old competitive instincts kicked in. If this was a race, Kennedy didn't want the United States to simply catch up to the Soviet Union—he wanted his country to win.

"I believe that this nation should commit itself to achieving the goal, before this decade is out, of landing a man on the moon and returning him safely to Earth," Kennedy had announced during his first year as President. Then, step by step, throughout Kennedy's years in office, the space program had moved astronauts closer and closer to the moon. In the midst of the troubles and fears that Americans experienced in the early sixties, the thought of a man walking on the moon was a welcome dream.

"You look up there and see the moon so far away," said one young woman, "and you think about how tiny the earth must look from the moon. Somehow, the thought of that makes all my worries seem so much smaller."

As 1963 drew to a close, Kennedy knew it was time to begin the task of campaigning for President again. He had been President for just over 1,000 days, and there was still so much he wanted to do.

"The pay is good, and I can walk to work," he often joked when asked why he liked being President, but the truth was that John F. Kennedy genuinely loved his country. He wanted another four years to serve the American people.

The South loomed as the biggest obstacle between Kennedy and reelection. While many white southerners strongly supported civil rights and would give Kennedy their votes, many more were determined to see him lose. One year away from Election Day, Kennedy decided it was time to head to the South and meet voters. Perhaps he could win over those who were still undecided about the issue of civil rights. Kennedy met with his aides in early November of 1963, and they all agreed that the President should tackle the biggest southern state first: Texas.

As final plans were being made for Kennedy's tour through Texas, security recommended that a bulletproof bubble be placed on the convertible that Kennedy would be riding in when greeting crowds. Usually, Kennedy agreed with whatever security suggested, but this time he did not. At the last moment, he had persuaded Jackie to accompany him on this trip. It was very rare for Jackie Kennedy to accompany the President in his travels, and Kennedy was well aware that most people would be more interested in seeing her than him.

"No, I want the crowds to have a better view of Jackie," Kennedy said with a grin. "We'll be fine."

CHAPTER 12

"Jackie! Jackieeee!"

Kennedy had been right. As soon as he and Jackie stepped off the plane at their first stop in San Antonio, the crowds went wild for Jackie Kennedy. All week, there had been great anticipation about what Jackie would do, what she would say, and, most important, what she would be wearing. The press snapped some pictures of the President, but they positively swarmed his wife.

"Why is it," Kennedy joked with the press, "that no one ever cares what Lyndon Johnson and I wear?"

Kennedy's personal assistant noted the size of the crowd at each stop and informed the President that he was doing pretty well. "However," he added wryly, "there's an extra 150,000 here for Jackie."

The trip to Texas was to be a whirlwind kind of visit. There was only an hour set aside for a speech in San Antonio, and then it was off to Houston and then Fort Worth. The Kennedys and the Johnsons would stay overnight in Fort Worth and leave for Dallas the next day. There would be a quick ride through the city to wave at the crowds, a lunch, and then the return to Washington on *Air Force One*.

As Johnson's wife, Lady Bird, prepared to leave the hotel that next morning, November 22, she noticed that her hands were shaking. Years earlier, when she had accompanied her husband on a campaign trip to Dallas, a group of men who had disagreed with Johnson's politics had shouted horrible things and spit on him. Now, Lady Bird had a bad feeling about Dallas. There might be something ugly today, she thought as she, Lyndon, and the Kennedys rode to the airport.

Kennedy's security team felt the same dread. More than once, Kennedy had been warned to stay away from Dallas—there was particularly strong anti-Kennedy sentiment in that city. Dallas had the highest murder rate in the entire state of Texas, and one in five citizens carried a handgun. The morning Kennedy was to arrive, the Dallas newspaper had run a full-page ad accusing the President of ignoring the Constitution. For all these reasons and more, security again suggested that Kennedy use the bulletproof bubble top on the convertible.

However, Kennedy waved off security's concerns. More than once, Kennedy had said that if an assassin was determined to shoot him, there wasn't much anyone could do about it anyway. Kennedy was not foolhardy, but he believed in living life to the fullest, even if there were possible dangers.

"He had no fear or premonition of dying," Kennedy's speechwriter, Ted Sorensen, once said of the President. "He did not need to be reminded that the life he loved was a precious, impermanent gift, not to be wasted for a moment."

When the President's plane touched down at the Dallas airport, hundreds of well-wishers cheered and held signs of support. Jackie was handed a huge bouquet of red roses shortly after she stepped off the plane. Just by luck, the flowers were the perfect accessory to the pink wool suit the First Lady was wearing. Along with the cheers, there were a few protest signs and an occasional boo, but all in all, the Kennedys and the Johnsons were encouraged by the warm welcome. It was an unusually sunny and mild day for late November, so Kennedy was glad he had stuck with his choice to ride through the streets of downtown Dallas in the open convertible.

As the President's motorcade entered the city, 250,000 people jammed the sidewalks, hoping to get a glimpse of the President and, more important, of Jackie. The roar of approval made Kennedy smile. For all of the worry and warnings that had preceded his arrival, Kennedy thought Dallas was turning out to be a wonderfully gracious city. Midway through the procession, the President spotted a small, sloppily printed sign: MR. PRESIDENT, PLEASE STOP AND SHAKE OUR HANDS! A group of waving children gathered around the sign.

"Stop the car for a moment," Kennedy called up to the driver. The President hopped out and shook the hands of the ecstatic children. As his car drove off, he could hear the children shouting excitedly, "It worked! It worked!" Only a block later, Kennedy stopped again to shake hands with a group of nuns.

At 12:29, the motorcade turned to drive through a small park named Dealey Plaza. Just past the plaza was an underpass leading to the freeway that would take Kennedy out of the city and crowds, and to the lunch reception. Jackie breathed a small sigh of relief. Things had gone so well. It was almost over.

Texas governor John Connally and his wife were sitting in the seat in front of Jack and Jackie. At 12:30, just as the motorcade was nearing the far side of the grassy plaza, Mrs. Connally turned around and smiled. "Well, Mr. President, you can't say Dallas doesn't love you," she said over the noise of the cheers.

Kennedy smiled back and waved at a child who was being lifted into the air by his father. Then Kennedy turned back to Mrs. Connally as if to respond to her comment.

He never got the chance.

The sharp crack of a gunshot echoed in the air. Kennedy clutched his throat and leaned toward Jackie. Blood streamed down his neck. At the same moment, Governor Connally fell forward in his seat. The bullet that had hit the President's neck had also hit the governor in his back. Then a second shot hit Kennedy in the back of the head. Because of the stiff back brace that he often wore, Kennedy was unable to duck. He remained upright, making him the perfect target for a third bullet. The first two shots may not have killed Kennedy, but the third one shattered his skull terribly, spraying blood and bits of bone everywhere.

"Oh no! No!"

Jackie Kennedy, in confusion and panic, screamed and then crawled out onto the back of the car, possibly looking for help. Scattered rose petals flew into the air as one of Kennedy's Secret Service agents jumped onto the trunk of the car, pushed Jackie back to her seat, and covered the President.

In the car behind the President's, one of Kennedy's aides stared at what was happening. The President's car swerved wildly and then seemed to come to a complete stop. For just a moment, the crowd near the end of Dealey Plaza watched in silent horror. Then, in a growing level of panic, shouts rang out: "He's been shot! The President has been shot!"

Reaching speeds of up to eighty miles an hour, the President's car raced to the nearest hospital, four miles away. Governor Connally had also been shot three times, but his wounds were not life-threatening. The governor's wife held her husband and calmly repeated, "It's going to be all right," over and over again. However, Jackie sobbed uncontrollably. With Jack's shattered head on her lap, she leaned over him, crying, "He's dead. They've killed him. Oh Jack, oh Jack, I love you!"

When the car reached the hospital, Kennedy's lifeless form was quickly placed on a stretcher, a few rose petals still clinging to his jacket. Kennedy's close friend and personal assistant, Dave Powers, rushed out of another car and ran to his old friend's side. When he saw Kennedy, he reached for his hand and began crying. "Oh my God, Mr. President, what did they do?" Quietly, he placed a jacket over the President's head so that strangers and reporters, now rushing up to the emergency entrance, would not stare.

For thirty minutes, a team of doctors worked on Kennedy, but there was nothing they could do. For a moment, his pulse returned, then it faded, and then he was gone. For the fourth and final time in Kennedy's life, a priest performed last rites on him.

"Eternal rest grant unto him, O Lord," the priest concluded.

Jackie, standing at the priest's side, added in a whisper, "And let perpetual light shine on him."

Back near Dealey Plaza, a thin, nervous man was seen running through the halls of the Texas School Book Depository, an old brick building across the street from where Kennedy had been shot. No one thought much of it. After all, the man was an employee there. But then, the man left work suddenly, and coworkers recalled something odd: Just that morning, he had arrived at work with a long thin package that he had claimed held curtain rods. Could it have held a rifle instead?

Police were immediately put on alert for Lee Harvey Oswald, the book depository employee. Within hours, he was confronted downtown, but Oswald shot and killed the police officer who approached him and then he fled to a nearby movie theater to hide out. It didn't take long, however, for police to track Oswald down. As they dragged him out of the theater, he smirked at onlookers and shouted, "Everybody will know who I am now!"

Across town, a bronze casket containing Kennedy's body was being loaded onto *Air Force One*. Jackie stood nearby, reluctant to take her hand off the casket. One observer noted, "The look in her eyes was like an animal that had been trapped, like a little rabbit—brave, but fear was in the eyes."

Barely two hours after John F. Kennedy had been smiling broadly and waving at the well-wishers in Dallas, his vice president, Lyndon Johnson, stood in the main cabin of *Air Force One* with one hand on a Bible and one hand raised, facing a federal judge.

"I do solemnly swear," Johnson began somberly, "that I will faithfully execute the office of President of the United States."

To Johnson's right stood his shaken wife, whose premonition about Dallas had been tragically confirmed. To Johnson's left stood the stunned Jacqueline Kennedy. Although aides had given her clean clothes to change into, Jackie refused to take off the blood-spattered pink suit. She continued to wear it through the flight back to Washington, amid the throngs of photographers that awaited her arrival, and as she wept with Bobby Kennedy at the airport.

"Let them see what they've done," she repeated.

Who was the assassin, Lee Harvey Oswald?

Years earlier, Oswald had been in the Marines, but during his time of service, he had become so fascinated with Communism that he eventually moved to the Soviet Union. While there, he married a Russian woman and then returned to the United States. Oswald had never been considered particularly dangerous, though he had been in and out of trouble with the law. During the time that Kennedy had been struggling with how to handle Cuba, Oswald had handed out leaflets that read HANDS OFF CUBA! and had been arrested for disturbing the peace.

Before the trip to Texas, Kennedy's security team had worried mostly about the President being shot or attacked by angry racists. No one would have guessed that in a city as conservative as Dallas, Kennedy's biggest threat would come from a Communist sympathizer.

"He didn't even have the satisfaction of being killed for civil rights," Jackie would later grimly point out. "Instead, he was shot by some silly little Communist."

In the two days following Kennedy's assassination, Oswald repeatedly denied killing the President. "I didn't kill anyone," Oswald shouted to reporters on his way to jail. "They're taking me in because I lived in the Soviet Union."

Americans wanted to know why—why did this seemingly harmless, two-bit criminal kill Kennedy? They would never get the satisfaction of finding out. Two days after Kennedy's death, when Oswald was being transferred from one jail to another, a man stepped out of the shadows, yelling, "You killed my President, you rat!" With that, the man, who would later be identified as nightclub owner Jack Ruby, shot Oswald in the stomach, injuring him fatally. An assassin had killed the assassin.

Almost immediately, some people began thinking that perhaps Oswald had not acted alone—maybe the entire assassination had been a plot that involved several people, each playing a part. Perhaps Ruby had been hired to kill Oswald so that the truth would never come out. After all, any number of people or groups might have wanted to see Kennedy killed, including Fidel Castro, Soviets, racists, or even leaders of organized crime. Some people even believed that the CIA had plotted Kennedy's death. These "conspiracy theories" are still being debated nearly fifty years later.

However, the world was not thinking about conspiracy theories on Sunday, November 24, as a two-wheeled horse-drawn gun carriage, called a "caisson," carried Kennedy's body to the Capitol Rotunda. The body would lie in state until the funeral Monday morning. Around the world, people mourned. "Our people are crying the rain down," one Irish newspaper reported. Radios in the Soviet Union played only funeral dirges, both day and night. Prayers were spoken in Buddhist temples in Tokyo. Church bells rang out in

Germany, and candlelight processions filled the streets in Switzerland and England and France.

In the United States, more than 250,000 mourners filed past Kennedy's coffin. People from vastly different backgrounds felt profound personal sorrow. Many cried openly on street corners, and strangers hugged. Obviously, not all Americans had agreed with Kennedy, but very few were left untouched by the untimely passing of this young, vibrant American President.

In his public tribute, Britain's former prime minister Harold Macmillan said that Kennedy's death seemed to "the whole of humanity, struggling in this world of darkness, the sudden and cruel extinction of a shining light."

On November 25, nine men from the five branches of the armed services carried Kennedy's casket from the Rotunda to the caisson that would take it to St. Matthew's Cathedral for the funeral Mass. Mourners followed behind the caisson in black Cadillac limousines. After the procession stopped briefly at the White House, the mourners continued on foot. Leading the procession was Jacqueline Kennedy, with Bobby and Ted on either side of her, their heads bent in sorrow. Behind them, over 200 people, representing ninety-two countries, solemnly walked the eight blocks to the cathedral. In addition, a million people lined the route of the procession in order to pay their final respects to their fallen President.

Throughout the three days since her husband's death, Jackie had maintained a dignified strength. No one had seen her cry or break down. But now, as the Mass at the cathedral began, John Jr. looked around sadly.

"Where's my daddy?" he asked. It was his third birthday that very day.

Finally, Jackie began to cry.

Five-year-old Caroline reached over and bravely took her mother's hand. "You'll be all right, Mummy," she whispered. "I'll take care of you."

Finally, it was time for Kennedy's casket to be taken to Arlington National Cemetery, a place so beautiful that Kennedy had once been moved to say, "I could stay here forever." Now he would.

Of all the heartbreaking images the nation and the world watched on that sad day, perhaps the saddest was the simplest. As the caisson left the cathedral to head to Arlington, it slowly passed Jackie and the children. John Jr. watched carefully. Then he stiffly raised his little hand to his brow and saluted his father farewell.

Jackie had prayed that perpetual light would shine on Jack, and so it would. At her special request, an eternal flame was lit at John F. Kennedy's gravesite. First Jackie, then Bobby, and finally Ted stepped forward and lit the flame. Since that cold November day in 1963, the light has never gone out.

Many writers and poets have tried to sum up what it was about John Fitzgerald Kennedy that captivated and inspired so many people. One of Kennedy's favorite authors, E.B. White, who wrote the children's book *Charlotte's Web*, certainly said it graciously when, only days after Kennedy's death, he wrote:

> When we think of him he is without a hat, standing in the wind and the weather. He was impatient of topcoats and hats, preferring to be exposed, and he was young enough and tough enough to confront and to enjoy the cold and the wind of these times. . . . It can be said of him, as of few men in a like position, that he did not fear the weather, and did not trim his sails, but instead challenged the wind itself, to improve its direction and to cause it to blow more softly and more kindly over the world and its people.

EPILOGUE ONE

ROBERT F. KENNEDY

"Thank God for Bobby."

More than once, John F. Kennedy had said those words about his younger brother, Robert Francis Kennedy. It was Bobby who had countered reporters with fiery responses when they had attacked Jack. It was Bobby who had thrown himself tirelessly into Jack's presidential campaign, working up to eighteen hours a day and sacrificing his own image in order to boost his brother's. It was Bobby who had argued so convincingly for a naval blockade instead of an attack during the Cuban missile crisis—a move that may have saved the world from World War III.

And when Kennedy was assassinated, it was Bobby who pulled the family together, comforted Jackie, helped with funeral arrangements, and made sure that his brother's private files and papers had been sealed and protected. When all of these tasks had been attended to, Bobby was finally able to shut himself behind closed doors and cry out, "Why, God?" as he sobbed for Jack.

Bobby was the protector, the one that family members turned to, and John Kennedy's most-trusted counselor and friend.

"Don't kid anybody about who is the top adviser," Vice President Lyndon Johnson had once said, rather bitterly. "Bobby is the first in, last out. Bobby is the boy he listens to." Johnson rarely hid the fact that he was annoyed that young Bobby Kennedy received more respect from the President than he did. And with President Kennedy gone, the nation—and even much of the world—looked to Bobby for guidance and comfort.

However, it had not always been that way.

"Aren't you even going to say hello?" an angry twelve-year-old Bobby Kennedy shouted at his older brother. Jack, who was already in college, had been so deep in conversation with a group of friends that he had not even seen his younger brother walk in the door. Bobby had been away for months at a boarding school, and he felt that his big brother could at least speak to him.

Jack just grinned and said, "Hello, Squirt," a nickname that Bobby was not fond of. In fact, Bobby was not thrilled with "Bobby." To him, it sounded girlish and a little too close to "baby."

After glaring at Jack, he stomped up the stairs in a huff.

If Bobby Kennedy was overly sensitive about being ignored, he had good reason to be. The seventh of nine children, he was a boy born after four consecutive girls. "He's stuck by himself in with a bunch of girls," his grandmother had once pointed out, shaking her head. "He'll be a sissy." And because Bobby was quite small and often had a fearful expression on his face, he was occasionally dismissed as a sissy by his older brothers, Joe Jr. and Jack. However, much more painful than that was the way Bobby's father, Joseph, disregarded his young son.

"Bobby was on the outside," a family friend once observed. "He wasn't part of the 'Golden Trio,' so his father rarely looked to be impressed by him."

The "Golden Trio" was Joe Jr., Jack, and Kathleen. Those were the three children that Joseph expected the most from, the three who captured the most attention from him. To Joseph, Bobby was the clumsy little boy who tripped over his own feet. "He's the runt," Joseph would often joke, often right in front of Bobby.

However, Bobby was determined from a very early age to prove that he was *not* a sissy, *not* clumsy, *not* a runt. When he was only 4, he stood on the deck of his father's sailboat as the family sailed out into Nantucket Sound. He narrowed his eyes and took a deep breath. Then, suddenly, he plunged into the cold water. He'd show them all—he'd swim or drown, but he would not be labeled a coward. Immediately, Joe Jr. jumped in and dragged his little brother back to the boat. But again and again, Bobby jumped in to prove his fearlessness.

"It either showed a lot of guts or no sense at all, depending on how you look at it," Jack Kennedy would later say about Bobby's determination.

"A lot of guts" might be the best way to describe the scrappy brother who would spend the rest of his life working to prove himself. Although Bobby witnessed the rivalry between Jack and Joe Jr., he was not interested in "beating" his older brothers. In fact, when he heard his older brothers fighting, he often went to his room and pulled a pillow over his ears to block out the shouting. Bobby simply wanted the respect of his brothers and, most important, the respect of his father. And throughout his life, he would continue to be unafraid of diving into dangerous waters to obtain it.

"A terror and a demon" is the way one of Bobby's classmates described Bobby when he played football. Like his brothers, Bobby had been taught that he must be the best and that coming in second or third was no better than losing. So Bobby was determined to make the varsity football team in high school. That wasn't easy. For one thing, Bobby had been shuttled around from school to school growing up, as the family moved around Boston and then New York, once to Europe, and then back to New York. As a result, his grades suffered, and he generally felt awkward around other students who never seemed to miss a chance to make fun of the "new boy." A friend of Bobby's during those years described him as a "bird in a storm," because, although he was fragile, he was determined to survive.

In time, Bobby discovered that he could fit in through sports. Joe Jr. had taught Bobby how to catch a pass, often throwing the ball as hard as he could to toughen up his little brother. No matter how much Joe's passes stung, Bobby did not complain. Instead, he'd ask for a harder pass. When he was a senior, his practice and determination paid off. Although he was smaller than nearly all the other players, he was possessed by the desire to win—and the desire to impress his father.

"You played a whale of a game," Joseph said to Bobby one night after Bobby had scored the winning touchdown. He even said it in front of the entire family. It was the first time Joseph Kennedy had ever praised his son, and Bobby would never forget it.

World War II brought both sorrow and excitement to Bobby Kennedy. He was thrilled with Jack's heroic efforts with the PT crew, and, along with the entire Kennedy family, he was devastated by the loss of his oldest brother, Joe Jr. Although Bobby was now a freshman at Harvard, he was itching to go to the frontlines and fight. But his father insisted on Bobby attending officer training first. Perhaps Joseph was worried about losing another son, or perhaps he simply didn't think Bobby, the runt, was soldier material.

"I wish to hell," Bobby bitterly wrote to a friend, "people would let me alone to do as I wish."

By the time Bobby was trained as an officer and ready to go into battle, World War II had ended. It seemed he would never catch up to his brothers in his father's eyes. He could never stand out as being unique or valuable. Playing football in both high school and college had been exciting, but it wasn't enough. Bobby longed to be needed.

When Jack ran for Congress and his entire family pitched in to help, Jack didn't expect much from his younger brother. "Take him out to see a movie or whatever you want to do," Jack told a friend, hoping to entertain Bobby the way one would entertain a child. After all, what could quiet little Bobby do to sway voters?

But Jack had underestimated the younger brother that he didn't really know. Bobby sought out the poorer, rougher neighborhoods, where voters often mistrusted a rich candidate. Bobby was not afraid to walk those streets and go right up to people and introduce himself. He sat down and talked honestly with the people who lived there—like them, Bobby knew what it felt like to be ignored or taken for granted. He even played football with some of the kids in those neighborhoods, knowing that a child's perception went a long way in winning the support of parents.

Bobby was often said to be both childlike and tough. He had a gentleness that made children trust him, and a steely strength that impressed adults. In the end, Bobby's contributions to his brother's campaign were incredibly valuable. His absolute devotion to his brother's success surprised Jack.

When Jack ran for the Senate in 1952, he would not underestimate Bobby again. This time he would appoint him as his campaign manager.

Before Jack's Senate race, however, Bobby Kennedy finally did something that no other Kennedy brother had yet done—he got married. Ethel Skakel was an energetic young woman who, like Bobby, was deeply religious.

She believed in Bobby one hundred percent, and for the first time in his life, Bobby became both self-confident and at ease with who he was.

In time, Bobby and Ethel would have eleven children, all of them living in a sprawling house painted in ice cream colors. Ponies, pigeons, goats, and even an armadillo played with the children in the back yard. And the yard also included slides, monkey bars, and a huge swimming pool. Bobby and Ethel's home was the picture of joyful chaos, perhaps the exact opposite of the strict household Bobby had grown up in. As a father, he took great pains to pay equal attention to every one of his children. Bobby never wanted any of them to feel as if they didn't measure up.

The same could not be said for Bobby's own father. As soon as Jack had won his Senate seat, thanks in great part to Bobby's hard work, Joseph Kennedy looked at Bobby and barked, "What are you going to do now? Are you going to just sit on your tail end and do nothing for the rest of your life?"

Hardly.

Over the next several years, Bobby would work tirelessly as a lawyer for the Senate's Subcommittee on Investigations. This was a committee that looked into crime and corruption. Along with other lawyers, Bobby worked to expose the gangsters who often used threats and violence to get what they wanted. Some men on the subcommittee feared these gangsters and mobsters—but Bobby didn't. Taking on the leader of the Chicago Mafia, Bobby looked Sam Giancana right in the eye and did not flinch.

"Do you stuff the people you kill into the trunks of cars?" Bobby asked coolly.

Giancana just laughed and looked away.

"I thought only little girls giggled, Mr. Giancana," Bobby said, tapping his fingers on the desk and waiting for an answer.

Many of these hearings were broadcast on television, and eventually the American public came to think of this younger Kennedy brother as the persistent, fearless one. He would do whatever was needed to get the job done.

In 1960, this was the exact quality that Jack Kennedy wanted in a campaign manager for his run for the presidency.

Thank God for Bobby. In his brother, Jack had found a campaign manager that other candidates could only dream of having. Unconcerned about his own image, Bobby screamed at campaign workers, shouted at the press, took on the difficult job of delivering unpleasant news, and handled civil rights issues so that Jack would not lose votes in the South.

When, after winning the presidency, Kennedy chose his brother to be attorney general, he did not do it to reward Bobby. He did it because he needed Bobby. He needed someone he could trust completely, whose intelligence and strength matched his own. He needed someone whose sympathy for the underprivileged and those who endured discrimination even surpassed his own.

For three years, Jack and Bobby worked so closely that some described their bond as one so connected that it was impossible to tell where one brother left off and the other began. Certainly, Jack had many advisers and counselors, but as Johnson had pointed out, no one compared to Bobby.

"There's been so much hate. . . . I thought it would be me."

Those were the first words Bobby said after hearing that Jack had been shot in Dallas. Bobby was as stunned as anyone, but, after the President's death was confirmed, there was so much to do. The little boy who, years earlier, had so desperately wanted to be needed, now carried the heavy weight of taking care of the family, the arrangements, and the comments to the press.

For some time after his brother's death, Bobby Kennedy seemed like a lost man. He was often seen out walking for hours in the fields near his house, wearing Jack's old leather bomber jacket. He would visit Jack's grave, even in the middle of the night, and kneel in the rain and snow to pray. He was disinterested in his work, and friends worried that he was suicidal.

"The twinkle in his eyes that had always made him a bit childlike was gone," one friend said. "Somehow, even though he looked older, he looked smaller."

Bobby continued as attorney general for a while under President Johnson, but, ultimately, it became too difficult for him to remain in that position. It's not too harsh to say that Johnson and Bobby Kennedy hated each other. They did not respect each other, and after Jack was killed, Bobby resented Johnson taking his brother's place. He was angry that Johnson would get credit for all the things Jack had been working on.

Meanwhile, Johnson had always thought Bobby was spoiled and arrogant and that Bobby had flaunted Jack's preference for him over the vice president. Johnson also felt that the younger Kennedy was too soft when dealing with foreign affairs. Johnson preferred military action over peace talks and embargoes. Once, when visiting Johnson's ranch in Texas, Bobby had gone hunting with the vice president. When the force of the shotgun's recoil had knocked Bobby down, Johnson had sneered at him. "Son, you've got to learn how to handle a gun like a man," Johnson had scoffed.

Bobby knew what the vice president meant—he thought Bobby was a sissy.

Nine months after Jack's assassination, Bobby stepped down from his position as attorney general. That same summer of 1964, Bobby was asked to introduce a short film about Jack at the Democratic National Convention. For nearly twenty-two minutes, the crowd clapped and wept when Bobby was introduced. Johnson may have been the presidential candidate, but Bobby had the nation's heart. Finally, Bobby spoke briefly about his brother and, in ending, dedicated a verse from Shakespeare's *Romeo and Juliet* to Jack:

. . . when he shall die,
Take him and cut him out in little stars
And he will make the face of heaven so fine
That all the world will be in love with night
And pay no worship to the garish sun.

Later that year, as the haze of depression around Bobby began to lift, he sought and was elected to the position of senator from New York. Bobby was a young senator in an era of youthful energy. The fifties had been a time of seriousness, Cold Wars, old leaders, and black-and-white images. Suddenly, the sixties were exploding in color, protest, and the growing power of young people. In particular, young people were against the war in Vietnam and *for* the rights of the underprivileged. So was Bobby Kennedy.

Over the next few years, Bobby became a symbol of this new energy of the sixties. He sat down with civil rights leaders and listened to their anger and frustration. He traveled to some of the poorest areas in the country and spoke sincerely with the children who lived there. And he spent time in poverty-stricken, war-torn countries where conditions were so horrific that Bobby was moved to admit that if he'd grown up in such a world, he'd "be a Communist, too."

In a trip to South Africa, Bobby witnessed apartheid—a fierce policy of unfair racial separation that had been the official policy of the South African government for nearly twenty years. Bobby spoke to black South Africans, encouraging them to fight against their conditions. "Each time a man stands up for an ideal," Bobby said, "or acts to improve the lot of others, or strikes out against injustice, he sends a tiny ripple of hope."

These ripples of hope that Bobby Kennedy continued to send out were growing into waves. Young people began to see Bobby as the great hope for the future. But why didn't he speak out publically against the Vietnam War? In 1967, more than 9,000 American soldiers were killed in Vietnam, and tens of thousands were badly injured. The war was unpopular, particularly with young Americans who were being drafted into military service against their will and were then being forced to fight. Everyone assumed that Bobby opposed the war, too. Why was he quiet on this subject?

"If you go against my Vietnam policy," Johnson had warned Bobby, "I'll destroy you and every one of your dove friends."

To go against the war would be to go against the President and the Democratic Party. Early in 1968, Bobby made one of the toughest political decisions of his life: He spoke out against the war. And amid the frenzied support that was now growing into a tidal wave, Bobby made another announcement that millions had been waiting to hear: He would run for President of the United States.

The African American poet, Nikki Giovanni, was a friend of Bobby Kennedy's. She worked on his campaign, and she admired him for being, as she said, "real" in spite of his being a politician. Perhaps this "realness," this genuine concern for minorities, for the poor, for the weak, is what carried Bobby successfully through the primaries. Perhaps his honest desire to show support for those who faced discrimination was what brought him virtually steps away from the White House.

However, on the night of June 4, 1968, as a crowd celebrated Bobby's victory in the California primary, one young man in the crowd did not admire Bobby's concern for minorities. In fact, this quality of Bobby's angered him. The man had seen Bobby wear a yarmulke, a Jewish prayer cap, to show his support for Israel. This man, Sirhan Sirhan, was a Palestinian who hated Jews. He watched Bobby address the crowd, and then he followed him through the hotel where the celebration was taking place.

"I'm not afraid of anybody," Bobby had said only days earlier, bringing to mind the scrappy four-year-old boy who had jumped repeatedly into the ocean to prove his courage. "If things happen, they're going to happen."

And on that June night, they happened. As Bobby passed through the kitchen of the hotel, Sirhan Sirhan stepped out of the shadows and shot a single bullet into the brain of Robert F. Kennedy.

For a while, Bobby remained conscious. Onlookers claimed that his expression was peaceful, childlike. Some heard him whisper, "Jack, Jack . . ."

But sixteen hours later, the third of the four Kennedy sons would also die much too young.

EPILOGUE TWO

EDWARD MOORE KENNEDY

"**My** brother need not be idealized, or enlarged in death beyond what he was in life, to be remembered simply as a good and decent man, who saw wrong and tried to right it, saw suffering and tried to heal it, saw war and tried to stop it. Those of us who loved him and who take him to his rest today pray that what he was to us and what he wished for others will some day come to pass for all the world."

Those were the words of the youngest Kennedy brother, Edward, at Bobby's funeral. His voice cracked with emotion as he said farewell to his last surviving brother. It seemed impossible that each of his three older brothers had died violently in the prime of his life. At the time, it seemed nearly impossible for him to move forward in his own life.

Edward, or "Ted," as he was known, had been in San Francisco celebrating Bobby's California primary victory when he had received the news of the assassination. Horrified, Ted nearly collapsed.

A friend who was with him at the time described his reaction as "much more than agony, more than anguish—I don't know if there's a word for it."

What word could there be to describe the tragedy that Ted had seen in his young life?

Only five years earlier, Ted had walked with Bobby and Jackie, leading the procession of mourners at the funeral of his brother, John F. Kennedy. Perhaps Ted had not been particularly close to either Jack or Bobby when he was a boy—Jack was fifteen years older and Bobby was seven years older—but as an adult he was beginning to discover the unique bond that Jack and Bobby had discovered.

Now, for a second time, the bond had been forever broken.

In typical Kennedy fashion, Ted was expected to mourn privately and with dignity, and then to move on with his life, taking over where the last brother had left off.

"Just as I went into politics because Joe died, if anything happened to me tomorrow, Bobby would run for my seat in the Senate," John F. Kennedy had said years earlier when he was in the Senate.

"And if Bobby died," Kennedy had added, matter-of-factly, "our young brother, Ted, would take over for him."

Ted had already been a senator for six years

at the time Bobby was killed, and he was both proud and happy to be serving in the Senate. But what now? Was he expected to run for President right away? Many friends and advisers told him to move ahead quickly and start making plans for the presidency—there was no time to waste! Still, another close friend, a senator from California, sternly said, "Don't even think about it. You must not allow yourself, ever, to think about you being next in line for this terrible treatment."

Ted knew what his friend meant—next in line for assassination. With loud advice coming from every direction, Ted Kennedy did what he and his brothers had always done to quiet their minds: He went out to sea on his sailboat. For nearly three months, the last Kennedy son disappeared from public life to think, remember, cry, and, somehow, come to terms with his loss as he sailed alone along the New England coast.

Then, one hot day in late August 1968, Ted reappeared.

"There is no safety in hiding," Ted announced in a speech. "Like my brothers before me, I pick up a fallen standard. Sustained by the memory of our priceless years together, I shall try to carry forward that special commitment to justice, excellence and courage that distinguished their lives."

Perhaps it would be possible to move on after all.

Ted had been the baby of the family. The last of nine children, he was adored by his older siblings, who often called him "Teddy bear" because of his cute pudginess and his lovable nature. However, as Ted had grown bigger and his older brothers had jokingly referred to him as "Muffins," Ted had not been amused. Sometimes it was difficult to be the last child. Because his mother spoiled him, he was thought of as a "mama's boy," and because he was the baby, his father didn't expect much from him.

As the family moved around, Ted attended a different school nearly every year, just as Bobby had. By the time he graduated from high school, Ted had been to ten different schools in the United States and England.

"All that moving around put me at ease with strangers," Ted would later say with a smile, preferring to point out the positive rather than the negative. And it was true. Years later, some would observe that Ted was much more of a "natural" than either of his brothers had been at showing genuine warmth on the campaign trail. Ted, perhaps, was more willing to let others get close to him, to make friends.

Like his brothers and his father, Ted attended Harvard University, where, also like his brothers, he tried out for the football team. He was, perhaps, a natural at football, too. Big, strong, and fast, Ted made the team his freshman year. Apparently also keeping with the Kennedy tradition, Ted did not do particularly well in his classes, however. In fact, he was doing so poorly in his Spanish class that he asked a friend to take an exam for him—the first of a number of poor personal choices Ted Kennedy would make over the years.

Ted's cheating was caught, and he was expelled from Harvard for two years. Not surprisingly, Joseph Kennedy was furious with his son. Apparently, however, he was not too furious to pull a few strings to get Ted appointed as an honor guard at the NATO headquarters in Paris, France. The United States was fighting the Korean War at that time, and Ted had wanted to be on the frontlines, but Joseph Kennedy, once again, managed to keep a son safely out of the action.

Back at Harvard, Ted became more focused, earning better grades and even earning a varsity letter in football, something that none of his older brothers had managed to do. In fact, Ted was such a good player that he was recruited by the Green Bay Packers, but Ted turned down the offer to play pro football.

Still, Ted remained the shadowed brother—the boy who was expected to finish school and have a decent law career, but not the son who would become nationally famous. Even so, Ted began setting his sights high. After graduating from Harvard, he studied at the University of

Virginia School of Law, standing out as one of the best students.

The late fifties were a busy time for Ted Kennedy. While in law school, he met the woman who would become his wife. In 1958, he and Joan Bennett married, and by 1967 they had three children: Kara Anne, Teddy Jr., and Patrick.

As with all the Kennedys, Ted became involved in Jack's run for the presidency in 1960. A friend of Jack's recalled that the youngest Kennedy was an "odd-jobs man." He picked up lunch, ran errands, and, on one occasion, read Jack's speech to a large crowd when Jack's voice gave out.

Perhaps the Kennedy family didn't see "Teddy" as a very important component of the campaign, but voters loved the youngest brother's energy. In Wisconsin, he made a daring 180-foot ski jump to attract attention before talking about his brother. The following summer, he rode a bucking bronco to pull in a crowd for a speech. He was not as intense and driven as Bobby, or as intellectual and glamorous as Jack, but his good humor and easy-going broad smile were, perhaps, a welcome relief to some voters.

When John F. Kennedy became President, he had to give up his job as senator from Massachusetts. And when Jack picked Bobby to be attorney general, there was only one person who could keep the Massachusetts Senate seat in the Kennedy family: Ted.

"You boys have what you want," Joseph Kennedy had said to Jack and Bobby. "Now it's Teddy's turn." Perhaps Joseph Kennedy had not previously considered Ted to be Senate material, but now that the position would be up for grabs, he wanted a Kennedy to grab it.

It may have been Ted's "turn," but at 28, he was not yet old enough to serve in the Senate (senators must be at least 30 years old). For two years, then, Ted was groomed and prepared to be a senator. He traveled the world to become better acquainted with foreign policies. He studied even more law. He visited towns throughout Massachusetts and listened to voter concerns. Massachusetts voters, of course, were supportive of the Kennedy sons, and many voters liked the idea of another Kennedy senator, but not everyone was sold on Ted.

"He's just riding on his brothers' coattails," some voters scoffed.

"He's too inexperienced. He's only running for senator because his father is making him," others complained.

Even so, on Election Day, Ted won the seat. He did not win by a particularly large margin, however. The narrow victory led Ted to worry that maybe he wasn't cut out to be in politics and maybe he shouldn't be a senator after all. Little did he know that, years later, he would come to be regarded as one of the greatest senators of all time.

Ted had been in the Senate less than a year when John F. Kennedy was shot and killed. Ted had been only twelve years old when his oldest brother, Joe Jr., had died in World War II—now an old nightmare seemed to be returning. Ted dealt with the loss by working toward passing laws that he knew had been important to his brother. In particular, Ted focused on the civil rights bill. Like both Jack and Bobby, Ted was quite passionate about ensuring equal rights for those who were discriminated against. It was a passion that would stay with him for the rest of his life. As a writer for *Newsweek* would later point out, "Ted Kennedy was at his best—at his most genuine—when other people were in trouble and feeling abandoned."

Just as Ted was coming to terms with Jack's death, he nearly died himself. In the summer of 1964, Ted was riding in a chartered plane on his way to a convention when he suddenly heard loud crashing noises. Looking out his window, Ted saw that the plane was skimming the tops of trees.

"It was just like a toboggan ride, right along the tops of trees for a few seconds," Ted later recalled. "Then there was a terrific impact into a tree."

After the impact, the plane turned cartwheels across an orchard. Both the pilot and one of Kennedy's aides were killed instantly. Ted survived, but he was badly injured, with a broken back and a collapsed lung. For nearly half a year, Ted would lie inside a metal frame on a hospital bed. Doctors warned him that he would never walk again, but Ted waved off their warnings and insisted that he would. Nothing was impossible.

"And I never thought the time was lost," Ted said of those long months in the hospital. "I had a lot of time to think about what was important and what was not and about what I wanted to do with my life."

When Ted returned to the Senate, he worked harder than ever to help the poor and underprivileged in the United States. That was important; that was what he wanted to do with his life. Then, just as everything seemed to be falling into place, the unthinkable happened again: Bobby was shot and killed in Los Angeles.

Ted may genuinely have wanted to "pick up a fallen standard" when he reemerged after Bobby's death, but for some time, he himself seemed to be falling. His marriage was in trouble as rumors began circulating that he was having affairs. He began drinking too much. Then, on the night of July 18, 1969, Ted made what he would later call the worst mistake of his life.

Ted had been attending a small party on Chappaquiddick Island near Cape Cod, Massachusetts, when he decided to leave the gathering with a young woman named Mary Jo Kopechne. According to later accounts, Ted took a wrong turn on a dark road and then ended up on a rickety bridge with no guardrail. In a horrifying moment, Ted lost control of the car as it veered off the bridge and landed upside-down in the murky water.

According to Ted, he dove into the water seven or eight times in an attempt to rescue Kopechne, but he couldn't get to her. Ted walked back to the party and, rather than calling the police, asked two friends to help him. When his friends could not rescue Kopechne either, Ted did something inexplicable: Without contacting any authorities about what had happened, he swam across the bay to his hotel and went to sleep. The next day, the car was pulled from the water with Kopechne's lifeless body inside of it.

Needless to say, many, many questions arose. In the end, Kennedy received a two-month suspended sentence for leaving the scene of an accident. Kennedy explained his actions by saying that he was in a state of shock and confusion after the accident, and he admitted that he had made a bad mistake. Perhaps Kennedy's sentence seemed too light, but as *Time* magazine would write years later, "He was sentenced to life under the cloud of Chappaquiddick."

It was a cloud that would keep Kennedy from running for President until 1980. Ever since Bobby's death, Democrats had urged Ted to run for President, but for a decade, Chappaquiddick had continued to haunt Kennedy's political dreams. Although he was repeatedly reelected to the Senate, Kennedy could not quite gain the trust of many Americans.

When Kennedy finally ran for President in 1980, his campaign did not go well. Many thought that Ted Kennedy was running for President only out of obligation to his family name. And perhaps, to some extent, that was true. When asked on *CBS News*, "Why do you want to be President?" Kennedy could not really give an answer. He stumbled over his words and suggested that it was what he was expected to do. He appeared uncomfortable with the very idea of being President.

Finally, the strength of his Democratic opponent, Jimmy Carter, was too much, and when Carter began pulling ahead in the primaries, Kennedy decided to drop out of the race.

"For me, a few hours ago, this campaign came to an end," Kennedy said in a speech to the 1980 Democratic National Convention after deciding to end his run for the presidency. "For all those whose cares have been our concern, the work goes on, the cause endures, the hope still lives, and the dream shall never die."

And the dreams Ted Kennedy had for the American people never did die. Although he would never run for President again, he focused all his energies on the Senate and on helping people in the United States who were often mistreated or ignored: the elderly, women, minorities, and the poor. During his nearly forty-seven years as a senator (the third-longest uninterrupted time any senator has ever served), Kennedy wrote more than 300 new laws and fought for the passage of many more. He helped women get equal pay for equal work, pushed to raise the minimum wage, worked to pass a law that would allow new moms and dads to stay home for a period of time with their newborns, and supported equal rights for gay Americans. In 2002, he voted against sending troops to Iraq, a decision Kennedy later called one of the best votes he ever made.

Perhaps the most important battle Kennedy fought was the struggle for good health care for *all* Americans—not just for those who could afford it. Kennedy had personal reasons for his ongoing commitment to this particular issue.

Ted's son Teddy Jr. had suffered from cancer when he was 12, and he had to have a leg amputated. He was given only a 25 percent chance of survival. Years of treatment and operations followed, but, against overwhelming odds, Teddy Jr. survived. Kennedy knew that he was very fortunate to have enough money to pay for all the special care that his son needed. However, it pained him to think of all the parents who were forced to watch their children suffer and perhaps die because they did not have the money to pay the often outrageous costs of health care. For nearly all of his years in the Senate, Kennedy pushed for health care reform.

He was still working toward this goal when he was faced with one of the biggest personal battles of his life.

In May 2008, at the age of 76, Kennedy was diagnosed with terminal brain cancer. He would be the only Kennedy son to grow old and die of natural causes, but he would not go quietly. In his final fifteen months of life, Kennedy returned to Capitol Hill to vote on bills that were important to him. He continued to work long hours in his office with, as always, his two Portuguese water dogs, Sunny and Splash, by his side. He made a triumphant speech at the 2008 Democratic National Convention in support of Barack Obama, and in that speech, he made one more plea for health care reform.

"This is the cause of my life," Kennedy told the crowd. "New hope that we will break the old gridlock and guarantee that every American—North, South, East, West, young, old—will have decent, quality health care as a fundamental right and not a privilege!"

As the crowd roared, Kennedy echoed his sentiments from the Democratic National Convention twenty-eight years earlier: "The dream lives on!"

In the spring of 2009, Kennedy threw out the first pitch to his beloved Boston Red Sox, and then he was seen less and less as the cancer weakened him. In his final few months, Ted mostly took to the sea with family in his old sailboat, *Mya*.

"The sea . . . there are eternal aspects to the sea and the ocean," Kennedy said not long before he died. For a man who had seen so much loss and pain in his life, the presence of something eternal and unchanging was a great comfort.

On the day Ted Kennedy was buried, his son, Teddy Jr., spoke about his father. Teddy remembered how he had felt when he had lost his leg to cancer when he was only twelve years old. It had seemed as if the world had ended and any hope for happiness was impossible. It was, perhaps, the same way Ted had felt years earlier when his last brother had been killed.

"My father taught me that even our most profound losses are survivable and it is what we do with that loss, our ability to transform it into a positive event, that is one of my father's greatest lessons," Teddy Jr. said with tears in his eyes. "He taught me that *nothing* is impossible."